W9-CIG-435

WITHDRAWN

NOTHING THE SUN COULD NOT EXPLAIN

ERRO DE PORTUGUÊS

Quando o português chegou
Debaixo duma bruta chuva
Vestiu o índio
Que pena!
Fosse uma manhã de sol
O índio tinha despido
O português

Oswald de Andrade
1925

PORTUGUESE MISTAKE

When the Portuguese came
In a heavy rain
He dressed the Indian.
Pity!
If it had been a sunny morning
The Indian would have stripped
The Portuguese.

Oswald de Andrade
(*Translated from the Portuguese by
Régis Bonvicino and Douglas Messerli*)

NOTHING THE SUN COULD NOT EXPLAIN

20 *Contemporary Brazilian Poets*

Edited by MICHAEL PALMER
RÉGIS BONVICINO
NELSON ASCHER
And with a Foreword by
JOÃO ALMINO

SUN &
MOON

CLASSICS

82

SUN & MOON PRESS

LOS ANGELES

1997

Sun & Moon Press
A Program of The Contemporary Arts Educational Project, Inc.
a nonprofit corporation
6026 Wilshire Boulevard, Los Angeles, California 90036
http//:www.sunmoon.com

First Published by Sun & Moon Press in 1997
10 9 8 7 6 5 4 3 2 1

This book was made possible, in part, through contributions to
The Contemporary Arts Educational Project, Inc., a nonprofit corporation,
and support from the Foreign Ministry of Brazil
and the Consulate General of Brazil in San Francisco

Cover: *Cosmos: um passeio no infinito*
(Cosmos: a stroll in the infinite), 1991
by Guto Lacaz
Frontispiece: Guto Lacaz
Cover Typography and Design: Guy Bennett

LIBRARY OF CONGRESS CATALOGING IN PUBLICATION DATA

Palmer, Michael, Régis Bonvicino and Nelson Ascher
Nothing the Sun Could Not Explain: 20 Contemporary
Brazilian Poets
p. cm — (Sun & Moon Classics: 82)
ISBN: 1-557713-366-2
I. Title. II. Series. III. Editors
811'.54—dc20

Printed in the United States of America on acid-free paper.

MICHAEL PALMER, editor and advisor for the translations, an American poet who currently lives in San Francisco, has published the following books and chapbooks: *An Alphabet Underground, For a Reading, Sun, Songs for Sarah, First Figure, Notes for Echo Lake, Alogon, Transparency of the Mirror, Without Music, The Circular Gates, C's Songs, Blake's Newton, Plan of the City of O* and *At Passages* (New Directions, 1995). His work has been translated into many languages, including Brazilian Portuguese. He has also translated from several languages into English and has taught and lectured at many universities in the United States and in Europe. In this anthology, he translated poems by Paulo Leminski, Régis Bonvicino, Duda Machado, Josely V. Baptista, Lenora de Barros, Frederico Barbosa, Ruy Vasconcelos, Angela de Campos and Claudia Roquette-Pinto.

JOÃO ALMINO, who wrote the foreword and was consulted on several matters related to this book, is a Brazilian writer, author of the novels *Idéias para Onde Passar o Fim do Mundo* ["Ideas on Where to Spend the End of the World"] and *Samba-Enredo* ["Samba Screens"], as well as of several books of essays. A diplomat, he currently lives in San Francisco, as the Consul General of Brazil and as a visiting Professor of Brazilian Literature at UC Berkeley and Stanford University.

Dana Stevens, a UC Berkeley graduate student in Comparative Literature, has translated contemporary Brazilian prose and poetry and is writing a doctoral thesis on the Portuguese poet Fernando Pessoa. In this anthology, she translated poems by Paulo Leminski, Duda Machado, Nelson Ascher, Arnaldo Antunes, Torquato Neto, Francisco Alvim, Age de Carvalho, Carlito Azevedo, Júlio Castañon Guimarães and Waly Salomão. She was also partially responsible for revisions of a preliminary version of this anthology in English.

Regina Alfarano, vice-president of the Brazilian Translators Union, teaches at the University of São Paulo. Accredited by American Translator Association, she holds a doctorate degree in English Literature, received a British Council scholarship for doctoral research work (England) and a Fulbright scholarship for post-doctoral work (United States). With many translations published overseas, her latest translated works include poems by Haroldo de Campos. In this anthology, she composed the Contributors' Notes and translated poems by Paulo Leminski, Duda Machado, Régis Bonvicino, Josely Vianna Baptista and Nelson Ascher. She and Dana Stevens translated the introduction and the contributors' notes.

Charles Perrone has published criticism in the area of Brazilian literature, has made translations of Brazilian poetry and has focused his studies on the poetry of song in Brazilian pop music. He is a professor in the Department of Romance Languages and Literature at the University of Florida, Gainesville. In this anthology, he translated poems by Paulo Leminski, Régis Bonvicino and Horácio Costa.

John Milton is a professor of English literature and translation at the University of São Paulo. Born in England, his translations include João Cabral de Melo Neto's book-length poem, "Morte e Vida Severina," soon to appear. He recently published *O Poder da Tradução,* a book on the theory of translation, and is now organizing an anthology of Brazilian poetry to be published in London. In this anthology, he translated poems by Régis Bonvicino and Ana Cristina César.

Martha Black Jordan belongs to the Tramontane Group of Poetry in Mexico City and is the author of *Hands in Water* (Poetry), Mexico City, El Tucan, 1994. In this anthology, she translated poems by Horácio Costa.

CONTENTS

FOREWORD

The publication of this anthology fills an important gap. In fact, very few anthologies of Brazilian poetry have been published in the US. Among them, one should particularly note those which resulted from the initiative of Elizabeth Bishop, Emanuel Brasil and William Jay Smith. These anthologies are, nevertheless, limited to poetry composed prior to the 1970s. Names such as Ferreira Gullar, Mário Faustino and the brothers Haroldo and Augusto de Campos are some of the youngest included in these previous selections.

It is my hope that the publication of this anthology will help increase the interest in Brazilian poetry in this country and open the gates to complementary projects. Subsequent anthologies are not only possible but indeed necessary, due to the diversity and comprehensiveness of contemporary Brazilian poetry. A similar potential exists in prose writing as well. In fact, the Portuguese language is spoken by some 200 million people world wide (more than French), and its highest literary expressions deserve a stronger presence in English translation.

The present selection starts where the previous anthologies stopped, with names associated with the tropicalist and post-tropicalist movement of the second half of the sixties, and covers other trends in Brazilian poetry since then.

To understand better the cultural context of the younger generations here represented, one should highlight two reference points—one far in the past, the other closer in time—regarding the tradition they received.

One is the major reference point for the whole of Brazilian

poetry during this century: modernism. Launched at the "Modern Art Week" during the politically turbulent year of 1922, it expressed, through the works of Mário de Andrade, Manuel Bandeira and Oswald de Andrade, among others, a rebellion against parnassian and symbolist movements, liberated the colloquial language, broke with the rigidities of metrics and rhyme and valued, often with wit and humor, the experience of daily life. It opened the gates for a vast spectrum of poetic expressions which included the oneiric images of Murilo Mendes, the mystical illuminations of Jorge de Lima, the metaphysical poetry of Cecília Meireles, the lyrical work of Vinicius de Moraes and the monumental and varied oeuvre of Carlos Drummond de Andrade.

In 1945, at the end of the Getúlio Vargas era (which had started with the 1930 Revolution and had included, since 1937, eight years of dictatorship) and at a time known for the reaction of some poets to the extremes of modernism, João Cabral de Melo Neto's poetry emerged as a unique neo-modernist expression which was anti-lyrical and concerned with form, conciseness and precision. An engineer or architect of language, he is generally considered the most important living poet in Brazil.

Cabral is one of the three great masters of Brazilian poetry throughout this century. Another is Manuel Bandeira, one of the participants of the Movement of 1922, who wrote a poetry of personal memoir, directed toward the small object of daily life. Finally, there is Carlos Drummond de Andrade, a poet whose work endured through several decades, covering a great spectrum of themes related to the subject of the modern man and his world.

As I first intimated, there is a more immediate reference

point, either positive or negative, for the younger generations of poets represented in the present selection: it is "concretism," a vanguard movement initiated in the mid-fifties, at a time of great industrial acceleration and technological development in Brazil. One can certainly build a bridge between the objectivity and visual imagery of Cabral's poetry and the concrete movement, which put new technological resources at the service of poetry and its visual impact. It should, however, be viewed as reestablishing a dialogue with the more radical modernism of 1922, against what was considered a semi-classicist and estheticist rigidity of the generation of '45. It postulates a rupture from narrative and the disappearance of the "self," and favors an atomized poetry across a graphic and visual surface. Concretism projected itself with great assurance and vitalism across both the national and international cultural stages. The movement, which initially counted in its ranks the poet Ferreira Gullar (who later launched neo-concretism) and which at some point in time encompassed works of other poets, such as José Paulo Paes, had as leaders and most faithful representatives poets Haroldo de Campos, his brother Augusto de Campos and Décio Pignatari. In addition, the Brazilian concrete movement was also important for the visual arts, as witnessed in the works of Mira Schendel, Lygia Clark and Hélio Oiticica.

The present selection starts with the generation following that of the concrete poets. This doesn't imply that those poets ceased to work. They have entered a dialogue with the new generation, and their work continues, through its own dynamics, to undergo important transformations.

Due to the criteria employed for the present selection, which is limited to twenty poets and basically covers poets who are today between 30 and 50 years old, a few important poets not included in the previous U.S. anthologies have also not been included in this one (José Paulo Paes, Sebastião Uchoa Leite, Adélia Prado, Orides Fontela, Hilda Hilst, Armando Freitas Filho, among others). Nevertheless, this anthology is highly representative of what has been produced in Brazil throughout the last twenty years, a period during which the country witnessed, in the mid-eighties, the transition from a military regime to a civil government.

The military regime which takes power in 1964 and radicalizes its authoritarian rule in 1968 is at the origin of the birth of a cultural generation essentially exiled in its own country. In the mid-sixties, the new poets are influenced by the musical outburst of Tropicalism, mainly in Bahia and around the musician Caetano Veloso. A less immediate but still important reference point for them is *Cinema Novo,* whose leading figure is Gláuber Rocha. Even though they maintain a dialogue with the concrete vanguard, they do not follow its rational and apollonian directives. Instead they fashion an informal poetry, marked by disenchantment with the present and lack of confidence in the future, where there is a place for nonrational expression. Their anarchic criticism targets not only the military regime but also the traditional or partisan left, reflecting the lack of closure of their poetry and their disbelief in the possibility of revolution. They are fundamentally concerned with the "here and now." In their use of colloquial language and their subversion of "good behavior," they view their movement as close or faithful to the spirit of modernism of the twenties. Of this group of poets, four are included in the present selection: Torquato Neto, a founder of Tropicalism, and Paulo Leminski, both of whom died young; and Waly Salomão and Duda Machado, both from Bahia, whose work has evolved throughout the years.

In the seventies, encompassing different tendencies which are at the origin of the work of several poets in the present selection and which again evoke the spirit of 1922, poetry offered an aesthetic and critical reaction to political repression. In those days, many young poets did not reach their public through the publishing houses. Poets would produce their own books in mimeographed form and would sell them on their own, often in bars and cafes. Their poetry expressed skepticism and an atmosphere of suffocation. Yet to this atmosphere the poets often reacted not by revolt, but by indifference; not with anger, but with humor and irony; not with any programmatic commitment, but with anarchic criticism.

A clearer, if nonsystematic, rejection of the technique of the vanguards occurs, mainly in Rio, with the so-called "marginal" or "alternative" poetry. In a colloquial and informal poetry of immediate experience, life and poetry are often considered one and the same thing. A major reference for this movement is the anthology organized by Heloisa Buarque de Holanda, *26 Poetas Hoje,* which would translate as *26 Poets Today,* published in 1976, and which included poems by Francisco Alvim, Antonio Carlos de Brito (Cacaso) and Ana Cristina César, as well as some of the poets of the tropicalist movement, such as Torquato Neto and Waly Salomão. A well-known poet from Rio de Janeiro not in that selection, but who deserves mention as close to this group, is Armando Freitas Filho. The present selection includes contributions from two of the country's most expressive poets of this movement, Francisco Alvim, whose work has survived these turbulent times, and Ana Cristina Cesar, a poet who left behind a consistent and important work when she committed suicide in 1983, at the age of 31.

Nevertheless, the anthology's main emphasis is on the generation which could be called, for lack of a better word, "Post-Concrete," a broad term which pays tribute to the importance Concretism has had in Brazil, mainly in São Paulo through the works of Haroldo de Campos, Augusto de Campos and Décio Pignatari, and includes the establishment of new parameters both in theory and in the poetic tradition.

When I say "Post-Concretism," I do not imply that these poets still work within the horizons of concretism. In fact, two among the best poets of this group, Régis Bonvicino and Duda Machado, for example, not only do not consider themselves affiliated with concretism but have ideologically broken with it. Even the most prominent originator of concretism in Brazil, Haroldo de Campos, has long departed from it. Still, concretism has been a major point of reference for this so-called post-concretism generation, which has dealt with a language experimentation whose origin can be found not only in the "concrete" poets, but also in Murilo Mendes, Drummond and Cabral.

With the process of democratization, there has been a broadening of perspectives without any clear cartography. Accordingly, in this anthology, there is a heterogeneous expression both in form and content. Some poems explore a mythic urban world, some a space of intimacy. An important characteristic of many of them is conciseness and a focus on the word as a thing. There are at least two examples of a visual poetry concerned with new media (Arnaldo Antunes and Lenora de Barros). Distinct from this approach, the synthesis produced by the poems of Josely Vianna Baptista, rather than structuring itself out of visuality, parodies it. In the case of Horácio Costa, who lives in Mexico and is an important translator of poetry from Spanish, the influence of the Spanish American tradition is evident.

Poets such as Júlio Castañon Guimarães, who is also a keen essayist, Carlos Ávila and Age de Carvalho are all highly representative of the new Brazilian poetry. And the vitality of this generation has been carried forward by the very new voices, as attested to in the poetry not only of Carlito Azevedo, but also of Angela de Campos, Claudia Roquette-Pinto, Frederico Barbosa and Ruy Vasconcelos.

In this anthology, there are poets from different parts of Brazil. They come not only from its main cultural centers, São Paulo (Nelson Ascher, Horácio Costa, Régis Bonvicino, Arnaldo Antunes, Lenora de Barros) and Rio de Janeiro (Carlito Azevedo, Ana Cristina César, Angela de Campos, Claudia Roquette-Pinto), but also from Minas Gerais (Carlos Ávila, Júlio Castañon Guimarães, Francisco Alvim), the South of Brazil (Paulo Leminski, Josely Vianna Baptista), the North (Age de Carvalho) and the Northeast (Waly Salomão, Duda Machado, Torquato Neto, Ruy Vasconcelos and also Frederico Barbosa, who moved when very young to São Paulo). Age de Carvalho and Horácio Costa presently live abroad, the former in Vienna, the latter in Mexico.

Paulo Leminski and Ana Cristina César are leading figures. The humor and irreverence of Leminski's biting vocabulary and the subtle strangeness of Ana Cristina's ambiguous "confessions" are, in fact, excellent examples of the varied and rich courses Brazilian poetry has taken in recent decades.

Besides being an outstanding poet of his generation, Nelson Ascher has made a significant contribution as a critic. He and Régis Bonvicino are actively involved in poetry reviews, having both participated on editorial boards of poetry magazines or literary supplements. Both have also consistently translated poetry, including contemporary poetry from the us. Mr. Ascher as well as Mr. Bonvicino are, therefore, excellent choices for editing this anthology.

I should add that this anthology has greatly benefited from having Michael Palmer, one of the highly distinguished American poets of his generation, as the advisor and editor for the translations. It has also counted upon the enthusiasm of poet Douglas Messerli, of Sun & Moon Press, who supervised the project.

JOÃO ALMINO

INTRODUCTION

Modern poetry in Brazil is no less peculiar than the country itself. Brazil is a Latin American nation, but this does not tell the whole truth. It might be more accurate to say that Brazil is actually the other face of the South American subcontinent, not so much hidden as it is unknown. The same might be said of the country's literature in general and of poetry in particular.

The Iberian Baroque, Italian Arcadianism, French Romanticism, Parnassianism and Symbolism: all have held sway in Brazil at one time, each manifesting itself in a highly original way. Our history, however, begins around 1922, during the centennial celebrations of Brazil's independence from Portugal. That year, an eclectic group of young writers, poets, artists and musicians, most of them from São Paulo state's coffee-growing high bourgeoisie, came together to promote a Modern Art Week at the São Paulo Municipal Theater—a fairly faithful copy of the Paris Opéra. French influence prevailed—Apollinaire and Cendrars along with Cubism, with a few touches of Italian Futurism.

The event left two important legacies: an ineradicable nonconformism in the face of provincial complacency, which took as its main aim to disprove any necessary link between social-political-economic underdevelopment and the status of the arts; and an increasingly fruitful relationship between the various branches of the arts. This contact was symbolically confirmed by the marriage of Oswald de Andrade, poet, writer, pamphleteer, playwright, critic and theoretician of Brazilian

Modernism (not to be confused with the distinct movement of Hispanic Modernism) to the painter Tarsila do Amaral.

In the 20s, Andrade wrote minimalist, anti-poetic poems and avant-garde novels, starting the Anthropophagic movement, whose aim was to swallow up foreign cultural influences and digest them Brazilian-style. He also wrote "Poesia Pau-Brasil" [Brazil-wood Poetry], a residual epic which, by mingling excerpts from historical chronicles and flashes of historical and geographical perception, redraws Brazilian history as an anti-epic, less by what is said than by what is insinuated between the lines. Andrade's concept of "anthropophagy" would be taken up in an original manner by the pop music of the 60s. However, let us not get ahead of history.

The initial movement of Modernism in the 20s introduced into Brazilian poetry a global attitude, incorporating broad cultural interests, irreverence, humor, and free verse. In addition to Oswald de Andrade, some pioneers included Mário de Andrade, Raul Bopp and Luís Aranha. Modernism's great *corpus,* and arguably Brazilian poetry's finest hour, came in the 30s, with the second wave of Modernists. The poetry of Carlos Drummond de Andrade, Murilo Mendes, Vinícius de Moraes and Manuel Bandeira, both individually and as a group, was equal to the principal currents of Western Modernism. The high quality of these poets is matched only by their sheer bad luck in having been confined to a readership, not only in their own tongue, but also in their own country, since they are exceedingly little known even in Portugal, a country whose poetic sensibility has taken paths substantially different from our own.

The poetry of the 40s, today almost entirely forgotten, represents a reaction against Modernist principles. One poet originating from that decade, however, proved durable: João Cabral de Melo Neto. In addition to refining poetic techniques, he provided a synthesis of the novel's most representative trends and concerns. Using a poetic art mostly inherited from Drummond, Melo Neto incorporated traces of Northeastern themes common to many novelists of the period, particularly Graciliano Ramos. Of course, his poetry was not limited to these concerns, and Melo Neto applied his method to a variety of issues, not least to a consideration of poetry itself.

During the following decade, Vinícius de Moraes, who had started his career as a poet nurturing rather vague metaphysical speculations interspersed with an interest in less universal, more concrete themes, began to mingle his interests with those of a new generation of popular music composers. Together they started a movement which would radically change the profile of pop music: the Bossa Nova. This movement, a confluence of Modernist diction with the urbanization and gentrification of rhythms, promoted a cooperation between so-called elite art (*pero no mucho*) and pop art (*ma non troppo*). This cooperation would last for a good quarter of a century, reaching its peak in the musical movement of the 60s, Tropicalism.

In a country where poetry is neither widely read nor taught, the status of Brazilian pop music is very sound, since every poet born since the 1950s not only stemmed from its roots but also, consciously or not, felt its influence. Any poet under the age of 45 who alleges otherwise is lying. That said, it should also be noted that, during this period, Brazilian pop music not only played a different role than pop music did in the English speaking countries or in Hispanic America, but also constituted a substantial and diverse entity of its own whose more lasting influence would not be circumscribed by political or sentimental manifestations, but would seek through its lyrics a continuity with the tradition of poetry as such. More recently, Brazilian pop music has lost its creative drive, and no longer exercises a meaningful influence over poets.

The 50s saw another movement which might be considered the third Modernist moment: Concretism. Led by Augusto de Campos, Haroldo de Campos and Décio Pignatari, its major drive may have been its placing of the intuitive program of '22 on clearer grounds—hence the importance placed by Concretists on critical and theoretical debate; on filling in any of Modernism's lacunas, including the restoration of published works, not least those of Oswald de Andrade; and on updating and fine-tuning the continuing international effects of Modernism.

From the following decade on, Concrete poets trod more individual paths. Haroldo de Campos turned to a kind of prose poetry and to the so-called neo-Baroque. Décio Pignatari moved between Oswaldian prose and poetry, both visual and verse, while Augusto de Campos stayed faithful to the movement's origins, developing and expanding its visual trends. Ferreira Gullar broke with these poets to launch neo-Concretism, later to embark on the project of poetry *engagé,* which he soon abandoned. Among the independent poets of the same generation (and therefore not included in this anthology), one might mention José Paulo Paes, Afonso Avila and Sebastião Uchoa Leite. The latter, without affiliating himself with Concretism or later on, with Marginal poetry, left a significant body of poems. These poems, almost all of them metalinguistic in nature, combined the erudition of a Paul Valéry with comic strips and American B movies, shot through with a nihilist critique of reality, specifically Brazilian reality.

This, then, is the background and environment against which the poets in this book began their work. It is worth noting at this point that the Concrete poets enriched the language with translations not only of modern poets (Pound, cummings, Mallarmé, Laforgue, Corbière and the Russians) but of earlier poetry (Provençal, *dolce stil nuovo*, the English Metaphysicals, and Chinese and Japanese classics). At least among poets, these influences ranked second only to those of Brazilian pop music. Through the work of these authors, the translation of poetry reached maturity and entered into a direct dialogue with living poets.

Contemporary Brazilian poetry stems from these precursors without being circumscribed by them. Apart from the distinct combination of influences that is inevitable for poets, individual personality and talent also play an integral part in their poetry.

Needless to say, during the three modernist "moments" we have mentioned, and even afterwards, much poetry was written which bore no resemblance to what we have just described. The issue was not an exclusive or exclusivist lineage, but simply whatever seems to have survived the test of time. Re-reading poets who did not join the mainstream is as melancholy as contemplating an outdated wardrobe. One example is much of the Marginal poetry of the 70s, which, whatever its limits, left us the still vital legacy of, among others, the work of Ana Cristina César and of Francisco Alvim. Their trademark informality is not without consciousness of more craft-oriented poets such as Elizabeth Bishop, Murilo Mendes, and Manuel Bandeira.

Indeed, one of the characteristics of Brazilian poetry of this century is the extent to which the success of individual talents has depended on their adhesion—dazzled or critical, playful or unwilling—to a minimal list of Modernist proposals. In fact, from '22 on, Brazilian poetry has fallen into one of two categories: Modernist or immaterial. It is hard to say now whether this division was fate or mere contingency: it is simply an empirical reality, verifiable by literary criticism's essentially rational criteria. This is an issue which neither theory nor the history of poetry has yet begun to examine.

For this reason, there is no common program for the poets in this book, no explicit consensus behind their writing. In fact, as opposed to the previous generation, these poets have shown little inclination toward the idea of belonging to a movement or school. Torquato Neto, for example, participated in Tropicalism, but soon afterwards abandoned it. In a very short span of time, Paulo Leminski moved from the geometric poem, which he was never to resume, to the exuberant prose of *Catatau*. The poets do have in common a set of concerns and poetic devices, however: there is the mainstream of an accepted tradition, as well as aims which, to a greater or lesser degree, all of them share.

Paradoxes

Paradoxically, poets from Brazilian Modernism on are unknown, owing less to their failure than to their success. Not only have they created many individual sets of poems (though that is surely true): they have created a literary universe of their own. Each one of them is, of course, connected with other universes, including those of French, German, Russian and Anglo-American poetry, but preferably acting through the whole.

There can be no *Weltliteratur* if a whole set of concerns and debates is not universalized. Thus, we are left in the odd position of having to define Brazilian poetry by what it is not.

From the 60s on, Leminski, born in Southern Brazil in 1945, built a diverse work addressing issues both from Modernism (20s) and Concretism (50s). In that sense, Leminski has one exemplary poem. In the beginning, a seemingly banal statement: that every poet starting his career thinks he will be the greatest, but by the end comes to little. So far, so good. But the key to the poem is embedded in questions of address more subtle than those of *vousvoyer* and *tutoyer*. In the first, optimistic half of the poem, the subject is "a gente," a kind of colloquial "we," but meaning "I" which becomes in the second, pessimistic part, a "we," indicated only by the verb, apparently the common first-person plural, but in fact the royal "we," symbol of the high rhetoric affected by the provincial elite. The poets Leminski invokes, as arguable as their sequence may be, only serve to illustrate the difference between the first "we" [a gente] and the second "we" [nós]. In short , the first is a kind of *yo el supremo* in a revolutionary state, whereas the second would be the same figure in exile, after the military coup.

In contrast with the exuberance of his prose and his personality, Leminski's poetry is notably concise. This concision is associated with voice and with the instantaneous register of existence. This kind of concision, as seen in the Concrete poems of the 50s, had turned toward radical definitions of language, giving little place to a more explicitly subjective register. Concision in the poetry of Leminski and Torquato, as well as in the poetry of many poets anthologized here (Horácio Costa is one exception) emerges as both a linguistic fact and as the possibility for subjectivity. If Oswald de Andrade was the inventor of the so-called minute-poem, we might go so far as to say that Leminski has created the instant-poem, mingling Oswaldian concreteness with the anarchic-colloquial diction of pop singer Caetano Veloso and the Tropicalism of Torquato Neto. Concision. Exposing ideas in few words. Haiku. If in Leminski concision is conveyed as brevity, originating from the pressures of existence, in another poet of his generation, Duda Machado, concision is present as accuracy, as precision. Machado and Leminski tread similar, but inverted, paths, the former departing from Tropicália and song lyrics towards a poetry of his own, completely different from that of Brazilian pop music. Leminski, on the other hand, a scholar after his fashion, continued to alternate between questions of high culture and non-systematic incursions into the world of pop music. Concision. The coincidence of three early deaths: Torquato, Ana Cristina César and Leminski. Three suicides, the first two explicit, Leminski's implicit in his daily consumption of alcohol and drugs. Three journeys begun during or after the war, three poets who produced their main body of work during the military dictatorship, which ended only in 1985, when all three were dead or dying.

Concision within extension. After all, there are haikus where words abound, where three verses are three too many, as well as epic poems from which no word can be subtracted without harm. The poem between prose and poetry: this is the case of Josely Vianna Baptista, translator of Lezama Lima's *Paradiso,* whose style could be considered a kind of Brazilian neo-baroque: rhythms and images, fashioned by the "feeling for the measure," in the words of William Carlos Williams.

Horácio Costa seems to be an exception to this scenario, following more openly the Hispanic discursive tradition, mediated through the American Beat generation. It is not surprising that Costa has lived in the United States and currently lives in Mexico. Wally Salomão brings prose and poetry together, with satirical and metaphorical overtones.

Arnaldo Antunes operates in Torquato's and Veloso's paradigm, highly privileging orality and visuality, as can be seen in his video-poem *Nome* (1994), which mingles pop music, electronic music, poetry and video. In this anthology, he presents texts which resume the instinctive-primitivist aspect of early Modernism.

Júlio Castañon Guimarães also writes concise poetry in the Minas Gerais style: lean, based on concrete facts and objects, often rough. This kind of roughness can be felt in the poetry of another poet from Minas Gerais, Carlos Ávila. Minas was the home state of Carlos Drummond and Murilo Mendes: mountains, silence and iron ore. Age de Carvalho is the one, among all the poets here, who practices a poetry of a more abstract nature. People and places are referred to fragmentarily; his imagination is often quite rhetorical, although his writings are short and sharp. Lenora de Barros' work covers urban themes, emphasizing the existing tensions of a large city like São Paulo, where she lives. While Barros' is a work close to plastic art, the poetry of Cláudia Roquette-Pinto and Angela de Campos (Rio de Janeiro based poets), in contrast, engages feminist themes maintaining a different, introspective dialogue with visuality. Carlito Azevedo, although a beginner, merits already some attention. There are two very new voices in this book: Frederico Barbosa and Ruy Vasconcelos. The general criterion for poem selection was how clearly the poet's procedures were conveyed.

It is well worth mentioning that nearly all the poets in this selection worked as publishers or collaborators for alternative journals in the 70s and 80s, such as *Navilouca* (Torquato Neto), *Pólen* (Duda Machado), *Qorpo Estranho, I* (Carlos Ávila), and *Almanak 80* (Arnaldo Antunes). These journals, along with *Código,* published in Bahia, acted as a laboratory where the impacts of Concrete poetry and Tropicalism were re-examined. At the same time, these publications served as a shelter for work with no prospect for commercial publication at the time. Another feature common to all the poets in this book: nearly all of them are translators. Leminski has translated, among others, Samuel Beckett, Lawrence Ferlinghetti and Walt Whitman; Castañon, Francis Ponge and Michel Butor; Duda Machado, Gustave Flaubert etc. These translations speak to a need to enrich a poetry which, strangely enough, has nothing in common with the poetry from Portugal or Hispanic America. The latter, discursive and deeply marked by Surrealism, never quite established its grip on Brazilian writers.

Once again, Elizabeth Bishop must be mentioned. She was to organize one of two Brazilian poetry anthologies for the Anglo-American world: *An Anthology of Twentieth-Century Brazilian Poetry* with Emanuel Brasil, published in 1972 by Wesleyan University Press (Middletown, Connecticut). It included Oswald de Andrade, Manuel Bandeira, Mário de Andrade, Carlos Drummond de Andrade, Murilo Mendes, Cecília Meireles, Jorge de Lima, João Cabral de Melo Neto, Vinícius de Moraes and Ferreira Gullar. Soon afterward, the same Emanuel Brasil oversaw the publishing of *Brazilian Poetry: 1950–1980,* also by Wesleyan, translating poets linked to Concretism, such as Augusto de Campos, Décio Pignatari and Haroldo de Campos, as well as some independent writers, including Mário Faustino and Ferreira Gullar, the latter a leader of the neo-Concretist movement.

Anthologies always run the risk of excessive partiality or superficiality. We hope to have kept these evils at a distance. However, it should be clear that other selections can and must be made. Among the young poets, there are many other promising names not included in this book, among them Beatriz Azevedo, Heitor Ferraz, Guilherme Mansur, Antonio Moura and Mércia Pessoa.

This is only our reading of what is most significant and representative in modern Brazilian poetry. Nothing the sun could not explain!

RÉGIS BONVICINO *and*

NELSON ASCHER

Tr. Regina Alfarano and Dana Stevens

TORQUATO NETO

COGITO

eu sou como eu sou
pronome
pessoal intransferível
do homem que iniciei
na medida do impossível

eu sou como eu sou
agora
sem grandes segredos dantes
sem novos secretos dentes
nesta hora

eu sou como eu sou
presente
desferrolhado indecente
feito um pedaço de mim

eu sou como sou
vidente
e vivo tranquilamente
todas as horas do fim

COGITO

I am as I am
a pronoun
untransferable
from the man I began
at the measure of the impossible

I am as I am
now
without great secrets beneath
without new secret teeth
at this hour

I am as I am
present
unleashed, indecent
like a piece of myself

I am as I am
visionary
and I live peacefully
all the hours of the end

Tr. Dana Stevens

A MATÉRIA O MATERIAL

3 estudos de som, para ritmo

arco
artefato
vivo
auriverde
sirv
o
a
fé
(ri?)
da fa
da, moça
in
feliz:

MATTER MATERIAL

3 studies in sound, for rhythm

arch
artifact
living
greengold
i ser
ve
the
faith
(laugh?)
of the fair
y, un
happy
lady:

arco
art & fato
vi-vo
auriver-
te,
sir v
o
a fe
ri D
a fa
da (in)
feliz

: vivo(a) o -
crefoto
cr&ivo &
não / o
qui-Z
a   o
rc
o
auriver ...
te eu
sir
v.o.
§ a raia-raiz

arch
art & fact
live ing
greengo-
l(a)dy
i serv
e
the (un)
happy
woun
de(a)d fair
y

                                    :living O-
                                    chrephoto
                                    I riddle &
                                    didn't wanT-
                                    o
                                    ar the
                                    ch
                                    the
                                    goldgreenY-
                                    ou I
                                    ser
                                    v.e.
                                    the roll-reel

a o

rc

o

arte   fa-

liz   &   vi.vo.

:

auriv/ver

te,

rai

Z

paris, 29-7/2-8-69

the a

   r

   ch

   art

         fali-

         city   &   i li.ve.

                                :

                                see-green/y

                              ou

                              roo

                              T

                              paris, 7-29/ 8-2- 69

Tr. Michael Palmer

LET'S PLAY THAT

quando eu nasci
um anjo louco muito louco
veio ler a minha mão
não era um anjo barroco
era um anjo muito louco, torto
com asas de avião
eis que esse anjo me disse
apertando a minha mão
com um sorriso entre dentes
vai bicho desafinar
o coro dos contentes
vai bicho desafinar
o coro dos contentes
let's play that

musicada por Jards Macalé

LET'S PLAY THAT

when I was born
a crazy, very crazy angel
came to read my palm
it wasn't a baroque angel
it was a crazy, crooked angel
with wings like a plane
and behold, this angel told me,
pressing my hand
with a clenched smile:
go on, pal, sing off key
in the happy people's choir
go on, pal, sing off key
in the happy people's choir
let's play that

set to music by Jards Macalé

Tr. Dana Stevens

você me chama
eu quero ir pro cinema
você reclama
e o meu amor não contenta
você me ama
mas de repente aquele trem já passou
faz quanto tempo
aquele tempo acabou

you call me up
I wanna go to the movies
you bawl me out
and my love doesn't please
you love me
but that train's already moved on
how much time
that time's been gone

Tr. Dana Stevens

ANA CRISTINA CÉSAR

SUMÁRIO

SUMMARY

Polly Kellogg and the chauffeur Osmar.
Rapid but intense dramas.
Photo romances of the conceptual heart.
Of the navy blue strapless dress.
I swallow insults but with sincerity.
Giddy with good sense.
Aerial of the square.
Artist of savings.
Absolutely blind.
Lust for the perhaps.
Mincing gait.
Water in my mouth.
An angel that registers.

Tr. John Milton

NADA, ESTA ESPUMA

Por afrontamento do desejo
insisto na maldade de escrever
mas não sei se a deusa sobe à superfície
ou apenas me castiga com seus uivos.
Da amurada deste barco
quero tanto os seios da sereia

NOTHING, THIS FOAM

To confront desire
I insist on the evil of writing
but I don't know if the goddess comes up to the surface
or if she just punishes me with her howls.
From the bulwarks of this boat
how I long for the mermaid's breasts.

Tr. John Milton

A história está completa: *wide sargasso sea,* azul
azul que não me espanta, e canta como uma
sereia de papel.

The story is complete: wide sargasso sea, blue
blue that doesn't frighten me, and sings like a
paper mermaid.

Tr. John Milton

é muito claro
amor
bateu
para ficar
nesta varanda descoberta
a anoitecer sobre a cidade
em construção
sobre a pequena constrição
no teu peito
angústia de felicidade
luzes de automóveis
riscando o tempo
canteiros de obras
em repouso
recuo súbito da trama

it's very clear
love is here
to stay
on this open veranda
night falls over the city
under construction
on the small constriction
on your breast
anguish of happiness
car headlights
slashing time
road works
at rest
a sudden recoil from the plot

Tr. John Milton

Quando entre nós só havia
uma carta certa
a correspondência
completa
o trem os trilhos
a janela aberta
uma certa paisagem
sem pedras ou
sobressaltos
meu salto alto
em equilíbrio
o copo d'água
a espera do café

When between us there was just
a letter certain to come
complete
correspondence
the train the tracks
the window open
a certain landscape
without stones or
alarms
my high heel
balancing
the glass of water
the wait for coffee

Tr. John Milton

TRAVELING

Tarde da noite recoloco a casa toda em seu
lugar.
Guardo os papéis todos que sobraram.
Confirmo para mim a solidez dos cadeados.
Nunca mais te disse uma palavra.
Do alto da serra de Petrópolis,
com um chapéu de ponta e um regador,
Elizabeth confirmava, "Perder
é mais fácil que se pensa".
Rasgo os papéis todos que sobraram.
"Os seus olhos pecam, mas seu corpo
não," dizia o tradutor preciso, simultâneo,
e suas mãos é que tremiam. "... perigoso,"
ria a Carolina perita no papel Kodak.
A câmera em rasante viajava.
A voz *em* off nas montanhas, inextinguível
fogo domado da paixão, a voz
do espelho dos meus olhos,
negando-se a todas as viagens,
e a voz rascante da velocidade,
de todas três bebi um pouco
sem notar
como quem procura um fio.
Nunca mais te disse
uma palavra, repito, preciso alto,
tarde da noite,
enquanto desalinho

TRAVELING

Late at night I put the whole house back in its
place.
I put all the leftover papers away.
I make sure of the soundness of the locks.
I never said another word to you.
From the top of the hills of Petrópolis,
with a pointed hat and a watering can,
Elizabeth confirmed, "The art of losing
isn't hard to master."
I rip up the leftover paper.
"Your eyes sin, but your body
doesn't," said the precise, simultaneous translator,
and it was his hands that trembled. "It's dangerous,"
laughed the skilled Carolina on Kodak paper.
The lowdown camera panned.
The voiceover in the hills, indestructible
tamed fire of passion, the voice
of the mirror of my eyes
denying all the journeys,
and the shrill voice of speed,
I drank a little of all three
without noticing
like someone looking for a thread.
I never said another word to you,
I repeat, I state firmly,
late at night
while I lose direction

sem luxo
sede
agulhadas
os pareceres que ouvi num dia interminável:
sem parecer mais com a luz ofuscante desse
mesmo
dia interminável

with no luxury
thirst
pricks
the seemings I heard in an endless day:
without seeming more like the dazzling light of this
same
interminable day

Tr. John Milton

PAULO LEMINSKI

O BICHO ALFABETO

O bicho alfabeto
tem vinte e três patas
ou quase

por onde ele passa
nascem palavras
e frases

como frases
se fazem asas
palavras
o vento leve

o bicho alfabeto
passa
fica o que não se escreve

THE ANIMAL ALPHABET

The animal alphabet
has twenty-three paws
more or less

where it passes
words and phrases
are born

like phrases
wings are fashioned
words
the slight wind

the animal alphabet
passes
what one does not write remains

Tr. Michael Palmer

PELO

pelo
branco
magnólia

o
azul
manhã
vermelho
olha

THROUGH

through
magnolia
white

the
morning
blue
sees
red

Tr. Michael Palmer

O ASSASSINO ERA O ESCRIBA

Meu professor de análise sintática era o tipo do sujeito
inexistente.
Um pleonasmo, o principal predicado de sua vida,
regular como um paradigma da la conjugação.
Entre uma oração subordinada e um adjunto
adverbial, ele não tinha dúvidas: sempre achava um jeito
assindético de nos torturar com um aposto.
Casou com uma regência.
Foi infeliz.
Era possessivo como um pronome.
E ela era bitransitiva.
Tentou ir para os EUA.
Não deu.
Acharam um artigo indefinido em sua bagagem.
A interjeição do bigode declinava partículas expletivas,
conectivos e agentes da passiva, o tempo todo.
Um dia, matei-o com um objeto direto na cabeça.

THE ASSASSIN WAS THE SCRIBE

My professor of syntactical analysis was a sort of
nonexistent subject.
A pleonasm, principal predicate of your life,
common as a paradigm of conjugation.
Between subordinated oration and adverbial
adjunct he had no doubts: always found an
asyndetic way to torture us with an appositive.
He married grammatical rectitude.
Was unhappy.
Was possessive like a pronoun.
And she was bitransitive.
He tried to go to the USA.
No way.
They discovered an indefinite article in his suitcase.
His moustache's exclamation point declined explicatives,
connectives and passives, forever.
One day I greased him with a direct object through the head.

Tr. Michael Palmer

um dia
a gente ia ser homero
a obra nada menos que uma ilíada

depois
a barra pesando
dava pra ser aí um rimbaud
um ungaretti um fernando pessoa qualquer
um lorca um éluard um ginsberg

por fim
acabamos o pequeno poeta de província
que sempre fomos
por trás de tantas máscaras
que o tempo tratou como as flores

once
we were going to be homer
the work an iliad no less

later
things got tougher
we could maybe manage a rimbaud
an ungaretti some fernando pessoa
a lorca a ginsberg an éluard

finally
we ended up the minor provincial poet
we were always
hiding behind the many masks
time treated as flowers

Tr. Regina Alfarano, with revisions by Robert Creeley

o pauloleminski
é um cachorro louco
que deve ser morto
a pau a pedra
a fogo a pique
senão é bem capaz
o filhadaputa
de fazer chover
em nosso piquenique

pauloleminski
is a mad dog
that must be beaten to death
with a rock with a stick
by a flame by a kick
or else he might very well
the sonofabitch
spoil our picnic

Tr. Regina Alfarano

A quem me queima
e, queimando, reina,
   valha esta teima.
Um dia, melhor me queira.

Whoever burns
me and, burning, reigns,
    take this game.
One day, cherish my name.

Tr. Regina Alfarano, with revisions by Robert Creeley

lua à vista
brilhavas assim
        sobre auschwitz?

        moon
did you shine like this
        over auschwitz?

Tr. Regina Alfarano, with revisions by Robert Creeley

apagar-me
diluir-me
desmanchar-me
até que depois
de mim
de nós
de tudo
não reste mais
que o charme

let me vanish
let me melt
let me fall apart
until
after me
after us
after all
nothing but charm
is left

Tr. Regina Alfarano

nada que o sol
não explique

tudo que a lua
mais chique

não tem chuva
que desbote essa flor

nothing the sun
could not explain

everything the moon
makes glamorous

no rain
fades this flower

Tr. Regina Alfarano, with revisions by Robert Creeley

um poema
que não se entende
é digno de nota

a dignidade suprema
de um navio
perdendo a rota

a poem
nobody understands
is worthy of note

supreme dignity
of a wondering
boat

Tr. Dana Stevens, with revisions by Robert Creeley

OLHAR PARALISADOR N. 91

o olhar da cobra   pára

                dispara
                paralisa o pássaro

                        meu olhar
                        cai de mim
                        laser
                        luar

meu despertar   despertar
meu amor desesperado   do meu olhar
meu mau olhado   despertador
                    meu olhar
                    leitor

PARALYZING GAZE 91

the gaze of the cobra   lies

belays
paralyzes the bird

my gaze
falls away
lunar
laser

my awakening   to arouse
my disarming love   from my alarming
my evil eye   gaze

my gaze
reader

Tr. Charles Perrone

DOIS LOUCOS NO BAIRRO

um passa os dias
chutando postes para ver se acendem

o outro as noites
apagando palavras
contra um papel branco

todo bairro tem um louco
que o bairro trata bem
só falta mais um pouco
pra eu ser tratado também

TWO MADMEN IN THE NEIGHBORHOOD

one of them spends his days
kicking lampposts to see if they light up

the second his nights
erasing words
from white paper

every neighborhood has a madman
it takes beneath its wing
not long till I can
be treated for the same damn thing

Tr. Regina Alfarano, revised by Dana Stevens

VERDURA

De repente
Me lembro do verde
a cor verde
a mais verde que existe
a cor mais alegre
a cor mais triste
o verde que vestes
o verde que vestiste
no dia em que te vi
no dia em que me viste

De repente
Vendi meus filhos
a uma família americana
eles têm carro
eles têm grana
eles têm casa e a grama é bacana
Só assim eles podem voltar
e pegar um sol em Copacabana

GREENERY

Suddenly
I recall the greenness
of the color green
the greenest there has ever been
the happiest hue
that makes me blue
the green you wear
green as you were
the day I met you
and you met me too

Suddenly
I sold my kids
to an American family
they've got a van
they've got the dough
they've got a house
and their lawn is fun
when back in Rio, now they can
go to the beach and get a tan

Tr. Nelson Ascher

FRANCISCO ALVIM

LEOPOLDO

Minha namorada cocainômana
me procura nas madrugadas
para dizer que me ama
Fico olhando as olheiras dela
(tão escuras quanto a noite lá fora)
onde escondo minha paixão
Quando nos amamos
peço que me bata
me maltrate fundo
pois amo demais meu amor
e as manhãs empalidecem rápido

LEOPOLD

My coked-up girlfriend
seeks me out at dawn
to tell me she loves me
I look at the shadows under her eyes
(as dark as the night outside)
where my passion hides
When we make love
I ask her to beat me
mistreat me deeply
for I love my love so much
and morning pales so rapidly

Tr. Dana Stevens

FRASES FEITAS

aí ele disse:
Não sou rico mas tenho alguns cristais
Viu que eu continuava sério
A gente não deve se sujar
por pouca coisa

SET PHRASES

so then he said:
I'm not rich but I've got some crystal
He saw I wasn't laughing
Why sully ourselves
for so little

Tr. Dana Stevens

FLOR DA IDADE

A tarde parou na janela
úmida verde
ela acabou de sair
nos despedimos sem tristeza

THE BLOOM OF YOUTH

Afternoon stopped in the window
green and wet
she just walked out
we parted without regret

Tr. Dana Stevens

LUZ

Em cima da cômoda
uma lata, dois jarros, alguns objetos
entre eles três antigas estampas
Na mesa duas toalhas dobradas
uma verde, outra azul
um lençol também dobrado livros chaveiro
Sob o braço esquerdo
um caderno de capa preta
em frente uma cama
cuja cabeceira abriu-se numa grande fenda
Na parede alguns quadros

Um relógio, um copo

LIGHT

On top of the dresser
a can, two jars, some things
among them three old prints
On the table, two folded tablecloths
one green, the other blue
a sheet, also folded, books, a keychain
Under my right arm
a black-covered notebook
In front, a bed
whose headboard has cracked wide open
On the wall some paintings

A clock, a cup

Tr. Dana Stevens

REVOLUÇÃO

Antes da revolução eu era professor
Com ela veio a demissão da Universidade
Passei a cobrar posições, de mim e dos outros
(meus pais eram marxistas)
Melhorei nisso—
hoje já não me maltrato
nem a ninguém

REVOLUTION

Before the revolution I was a professor
With it came my dismissal from the University
I began to demand positions, from myself and others
(my parents were Marxists)
I've grown better in this—
today I no longer mistreat myself
or anyone else

Tr. Dana Stevens

A PEDRA

Árvores me atropelam
folhas e galhos dentro de mim,
vazio de tudo o que sou
verifico que os vegetais, como as pedras,
apodrecem

THE STONE

Trees crush me
leaves and branches inside me,
void of all that I am
I can confirm that plants, like stones,
go rotten

Tr. Dana Stevens

DUDA MACHADO

CIRCUNAVEGAÇÃO

verbo que move o som
e outros sentidos

pacto
com o silêncio

colheita
de uma densa devastação

milimétrica medida
sopro súbito

monólogo
ao vento

manufraturada
flora de filamentos

fio que contém
seu próprio precipício

rio de todas as águas
a cada mergulho renascido

corpo-a-corpo
e inteira mente

CIRCUMNAVIGATION

verb that moves sound
and other senses

pact with silence

harvest
of a dense devastation

millimetric measure
sudden whisper

monologue
in the wind

manufractured
flora of filaments

thread that contains
its own precipice

river of all waters
at every dive revived

hand-to-hand
whole heartedly

Tr. Michael Palmer
Previously unpublished

IMAGEM DE UM JARDIM

baque de pétalas
emudece o ar

jardim perfeito
onde se anula a tarde
jardim sem erro

jardim alheio
a qualquer idílio
ou atrocidade

THE IMAGE OF A GARDEN

freefall of petals
hushes the air

perfect garden
where afternoon cancels itself
error-free garden

garden detached
from any idyll
or atrocity

Tr. Regina Alfarano

VISÃO AO AVESSO

neon insone
esquinas frigorífico
na madrugada
drogada
céu e asfalto
se ombreiam
exaustos
a uma canto
travesti e pivete
apressam um trato
:déjà vu
restos
pano rápido

INSIDE-OUT VISION

sleepless neon
icebox corners
in the drugged
dawn
sky and asphalt
exhausted
lean on each other
in the shadows
transvestite and street kid
strike a deal
:déjà vu
remnants
a quick rag

Tr. Dana Stevens

ÁLBUM

velocidade

    de sóis
    árvores
    corpos

floração

    abrupta
    de agoras
    tão êxtase

manhãs

    atravessando
noites
na mesma

    frase-brisa

grãos

    arrebatados
    ao sal do mar
    dor dourada
    atordoada alegria

poros

    abertos
    ao ideal

ALBUM

speed

     of suns
     trees
     bodies

blossoming

     of nows
     abrupt
     such ecstasy

mornings

     crossing

nights

     along the same
     breeze-phrase

grains

     grasped
     from the sea's salt
     gilded grief
     dazed gladness

pores

     open
     to the ideal

canções

que me adolescem
e mentem

songs

        that adolesce me
        and lie

Tr. Regina Alfarano

ACONTECIMENTO

Para Augusto de Campos

qualquer,
algum ninguém

um outro
que
por sua vez

....

miragem
de reflexos espelhados

ponto
de interseção do real

foi

está escrito

HAPPENING

for Augusto de Campos

anybody,
some nobody

someone else
who
in turn

....

mirage
of mirrored reflections

point
of intersection of the real

it was

it is written

Tr. Regina Alfarano

TEATRO AMBULANTE

Há três anos, representavam a mesma peça. O sucesso era tão grande e tantos os pedidos vindos de cidades do interior, que resolveram excursionar. Mas as viagens, ao contrário do que esperavam, iam acentuando ainda mais o cansaço e a rotina daquelas representações sempre idênticas. Para aliviar-se, os atores foram aumentando cada vez mais os trechos improvisados até que, pouco a pouco, a história e as personagens começaram a se alterar. Por fim, a peça se transformou. Mas a platéia não dava mostras de reparar naquela completa mudança. Ninguém reclamava e o público aceitava entusiasmado o outro drama representado e a presença daqueles atores famosos. Estes sentiam-se revigorados e o segredo da metamorfose atuava como um pacto a fortalecer a ligação entre eles.

Uma noite, passado algum tempo, sem que pudessem compreender ou controlar o que acontecia no palco, as palavras e os gestos que executavam, começaram a tornar-se alheios, irreconhecíveis. No segundo ato, todo o elenco estava assustado e atordoado. No entanto, no momento de cada réplica ou ação, o pânico desaparecia. Terminado o espetáculo, o público aplaudiu com o entusiasmo de sempre. Nos camarins, os atores mal conseguiam se entreolhar. Só mais tarde quando jantavam no restaurante do hotel, é que se sentiram capazes de reconhecer com excitação que haviam seguido diálogo por diálogo, cena por cena, a peça original, abandonada algum tempo atrás.

TRAVELING THEATER

They had been performing the same play for three years. It was so successful, and the requests from country towns so many, that they decided to hit the road. Contrary to expectation, though, these trips only added to the exhaustion and routine of the always identical performances. By way of relief, the actors started improvising more and more until, little by little, the story and the characters began to change. In the end, the play underwent a transformation. But the audience did not seem to notice this complete change. No one complained and the spectators enthusiastically accepted the other play being performed, as well as the participation of such renowned actors, who felt reinvigorated. The secret metamorphosis acted like a pact to strengthen the liaison among them.

Some time had gone by when one night, unable to understand or control what took place on stage, the words uttered or the gestures made, the actors began to find each other strange, unrecognizable. By the second act, the whole cast was scared and bewildered. With each new line or action, though, the panic vanished. When the performance was over, the audience applauded as enthusiastically as always. In the dressing rooms, the actors could hardly look at each other. Only later, over dinner at the hotel restaurant, did they realize, with excitement, that they had followed every dialogue, every scene, from the original play abandoned some time back.

Tr. Regina Alfarano, revised by Dana Stevens

ALMANAQUE

I

A matéria das estrelas
A primeira incógnita matemática

O que as ondas propagam
O mais leve dos átomos

A unidade das distâncias cósmicas
O corpo vegetativo das algas

O círculo que gira sobre si mesmo
A forma definitiva do inseto

O resultado da decomposição da luz
A temperatura do sangue nos reptéis

A função do nó
O que não é absoluto no ciclo

ALMANAC

I

The matter of stars
The initial mathematical unknown

What waves propagate
The lightest of atoms

The unity of cosmic distances
The vegetal body of the algae

The circle that spins around itself
The insect's definitive shape

The result of light's decomposition
The temperature of blood in reptiles

The function of the knot
The nonabsolute in the cycle

II

A forma da curva
O estado em que não há mais peso

Os condutos do sangue
A massa invisível do universo

A camada sob a crosta terrestre
O último ato do escorpião

Os olhos dos insetos
O ponto do céu acima do observador

A energia condensada
A vegetação das alturas

A curva quadrática
O fim do labirinto

II

The shape of the curve
The state in which there is no more weight

The ducts of the blood
The invisible mass of the universe

The layer beneath the earth's crust
The scorpion's final act

The eyes of insects
The point in the sky beyond the observer

Energy condensed
The vegetation on the heights

The quadratic curve
The end of the labyrinth

Tr. Michael Palmer
Previously unpublished

WALY SALOMÃO

MINHA ALEGRIA

minha alegria permanece eternidades soterrada
e só sobe para a superfície
através do tubos de filtros alquímicos e não da causalidade natural.
ela é filha bastarda do desvio e da desgraça,
minha alegria: um diamante gerado pela combustão,
como rescaldo final de incêndio.

MY JOY

My joy spends eternities buried
and only rises to the surface
through tubes of alchemical filters, not by natural causes.
She is the bastard daughter of waywardness and disgrace,
my joy: a diamond generated by combustion,
like the smoldering remains of an inferno.

Tr. Dana Stevens

MEIA-ESTAÇÃO

Presságios nas flores abertas dos junquilhos;
                    abertas, justamente, hoje de manhã.
O arco-íris e seu sortilégio,
                    justamente, hoje de manhã.
Folhas de figueiras levitantes, aéreas.
A baba epiléptica do mar hermafrodita:
            macho lambendo a areia da praia arreganhada;
           fêmea singrada por navios duros,
                    de ferros e aços,
           e seu mostruário-monstruário de mastros.
Tarda a vir o outono este ano,
                o verão não quer se despedir.
Um vento quente passa e acorda
              os feitiços e as promessas do verão inteiro.
Escrever assim é romantizar o vento quente que passa
              a lembrar somente
que é o vento quente e desaforado
a passar uma lixa grossa,
sobre a cidade, os seres e as coisas.

Vento bêbado de amnésia e desmemória,
incapaz de verão ou outono ter por nome próprio,
trafega indiferente à nossa tradição ibérica
que exige para tudo registro e certidão,
pagamento de estampilha ou selo do tesouro,
aval e avalista,

HALF-SEASON

Auguries in the jonquil flowers;

                              opened, precisely, this morning.

The rainbow and its witchcraft,

                              precisely, this morning.

Fig-tree leaves levitating, airborne.

The epileptic drool of a hermaphrodite sea:

                      the male licking the split sand of the beach;

                      the female navigated by hard boats,

                                by iron and steel,

                      and the monster-masters of masts.

Autumn is late this year,

                      summer won't say goodbye.

A warm wind passes and wakens

                        the spells and promises of an entire summer.

To write this way is to romanticize the warm wind that passes

                      remembering only

that it is the warm and insolent wind

dragging rough sandpaper

across the city, its beings and things.

A wind drunk with amnesia and unremembering,

unnameable either as summer or autumn,

traverses indifferently our Iberian tradition,

which insists that everything be registered, certified,

stamped or sealed by the treasury,

bond and bondsman,

reconhecimento de firma
por tabelião em cartório.
Além do estilo—imperativo categórico—do nosso arquétipo
de tabelião perfunctório

(parente lusitano-brasileiro do literalista pedante de Miss
Marianne Moore)

cujo breviário reza:

"Lavro e dou fé ... é verão."
Ou
"Lavro e dou fé ... é outono."

                    the firm's recognition
                        in the office of a notary public.
Not to mention the style—a categorical imperative—of our
            archetype of the perfunctory office

                    (a Luso-Brazilian relation of Miss
Marianne Moore's pedant literalist)

                        whose breviary prays:

"I hereby bear witness… it's summer."
Or
"I hereby bear witness … it's autumn."

Tr. Dana Stevens

DOMINGO DE RAMOS

I

O indesejado das gentes entrou, enfim, na cidade.
Seu peito é só cavidade e espinho encravado,
cacto do deserto das cercanias,
torpor de quem se sente aplicado por cicuta
ou mordido de cobra.

O que, convenhamos, lhe dá um ar desapegado
das coisas triviais
e acresce seu charme
paradoxal

perante o populacho.

A cidade é uma nebulosa de sonho:
tempos e lugares diversos embaralhados,
tantas glórias e hosanas, tantos pedidos de empregos,
partidos, facções, crimes organizados, júbilos e adulações.

Uma sensação de déjà vu
que murcha qualquer frescor
na idade madura.

PALM SUNDAY

I

He, the least wanted by all, has finally entered the city.
His chest is nothing but cavity and embedded thorns,
desert cactus of the outskirts,
torpor of one who feels drugged by hemlock
or snakebite.

Which, we agree, lends him a detached air

                                 from trivial things
and adds to his paradoxical
                      charm

                              in the eyes of the populace.

The city nebulous like a dream:
various times and places jumbled up,
so many glories and hosannas, so many requests for jobs,
parties, factions, organized crime, jubilees, adulations.

A sensation of déjà vu
                      withering any freshness
                          in its ripe age.

II

Assim falava o antecessor:
"O poeta é um ressentido e o mais são nuvens."
Assim ele, aqui, fala:
Os ressentimentos esfiapados

                são como nuvens esgarçadas.

Campo aberto,
ele vira uma câmara de ecos.
Câmara de ecos:
a substância do próprio tutano tornada citação.

Aprende a palidez altiva
e sorriso aloof
de quem compreende as variações dos ventos da mídia.
Estas qualidades ele supõe ter importado de Stendhal
e de Emerson,
já de Drummond ele assimila uma certa qualidade esconsa,
retalho daqui, recorte dali,
etcetera et caterva.

Ele: o amalgâmico
             o filho das fusões
                        o amante das algaravias
o sem pureza.

Como compor, com semelhante *melting pot,*
uma inteireza de homem
que caiba no anúncio "Ecce Homo"?

II

Here's how the antecedent spoke:
"The poet is resentful and the rest are clouds."
This is how he speaks here:
Frayed resentments

                  are like shredded clouds.

Open field,
he becomes an echo-chamber.
Echo-chamber:
the essence of the marrow itself has become quotation.

He learns the lofty pallor
and aloof smile
of one who understands the media's fickle winds.
These qualities he believes borrowed from Stendhal
and Emerson,
while from Drummond he draws a certain obliqueness,
a morsel here, a snippet there,
et cetera et caterva.

He: the amalgamated

                  the son of fusions

                            the lover of gibberish
the impure.

How to compose, with such a melting pot,
the entirety of a man
to fit the billing "Ecce Homo"?

III

Hoje é
Palm Sunday,
uma boa oportunidade para sobrevoar
de helicóptero:

os manguezais de esgotos negros e garças brancas,
os morros
de parcas palmas de palmeiras
e muito capim colonião
—o capim colonião ao vento parece uma cabeleira
encharcada de gel—
as praias
onde E L E simula
                        —através das leis do Livro do Caos—
o delírio demiúrgico
de que as hélices do helicóptero são as provocadoras
                                        das ondas do mar.

Palm Sunday.
Dentro do helicóptero
                    lá em cima
o diabo recorda-lhe, então, um conto de Sartre,
sobre Erostrato, o piromaníaco,
que adorava olhar os homens
bem do alto
como se fossem
formiguinhas.

III

Today is
Palm Sunday,
a good opportunity to fly over
by helicopter:

the mango groves with black gutters and white herons
the hills
the parched palms of palm-trees
and lots of crabgrass
—the crabgrass in the wind is like hair
soaked in gel—
the beaches
where HE fakes
                              —through the laws of the Book of Chaos—
the demiurgical delirium
that the helicopter's blades are what provokes
the ocean's waves.

Palm Sunday.
Inside the helicopter
                              there on high
the devil then reminds him of a story by Sartre,
about Erostratus, the pyromaniac,
who loved to watch men
from way up high:
they looked like
tiny ants.

Tr. Dana Stevens

JÚLIO CASTAÑON GUIMARÃES

GEOGRAFIA

sombras ancestrais
claras manhãs
em que margem?
ainda que a memória esbata as horas
o que há são espaços perdidos
uma casa
uma viagem
cabelos soltos em minhas mãos

GEOGRAPHY

ancestral shadows
bright mornings
what margin?
while memory dilutes the hours
what there are are lost spaces
a house
a trip
hair unbound in my hands

Tr. Dana Stevens

SEM TÍTULO, ÓLEO SOBRE TELA, 70 × 50 cm

quando, desfeitos os
nós da representação
contra si a imagem
investe, pouco resta
além da indagação
cínica ou retórica:
que imagem elide
sua crua corrupção

UNTITLED, OIL ON CANVAS, 70 × 50 cm

when, the knots of
representation undone,
the image weighs
against itself, little is left
beyond cynical
or rhetorical inquiry:
what image annuls
this raw corruption

Tr. Dana Stevens

O QUE SE PERDEU?

os cabelos de teu peito
nas tardes de domingo

nenhuma imagem
nenhuma estratégia

perdeu-se este poema
nu ardorosamente nu
e vivo e aceso
na ponta da língua

por entre tuas pernas

WHAT WAS LOST?

the hairs of your chest
on sunday afternoons

no image
no strategy

this poem was lost
naked, ardently naked
alive and lit
on the tongue's tip

between your legs

Tr. Dana Stevens

No horizonte, irresoluções. As tentativas cumulam incertezas, mas mesmo pontuações (talvez) sem propósito desenham ritmos; organizam-se séries de razões equívocas e desatenções; destroços de procedimentos, de exigências e de métodos emergem : mal disfarçado rigor resiste—matéria, trama, viagem, diário.

On the horizon, irresolutions. Attempts accumulate uncertainties, but even pointless (perhaps) punctuations sketch rhythms; set up series of dubious reasons and inattentions;expose the wreckage of procedures, requirements and methods: barely disguised, rigor resists—matter, plot, journey, journal.

Tr. Dana Stevens

LENORA DE BARROS

A CIDADE ÁCIDA

a cidade
ácida
asfixia

oxida
a palavra
poesia

o poema vem
de outros ares
de outros óxidos
e oxigênios

infiltra a seco
a umidade fria

o

pingue
pongue
oculto

que ali mina
gota a gota

o som sopro
do sentido
vida

ACID CITY

the a-
cid city
asphyxiates

oxidizes
the word
poetry

the poem comes
from other airs
from other oxides
and oxygens

dry infiltration
of cold humidity

the

secret
ping
pong

undermining
drop by drop

the soughing sound
of sense
life

Tr. Michael Palmer
Previously unpublished

há   **há**   vida   **vida**

onde   **onde**   a   **a**   vida   **vida**

acontece   **acontece**

o que   **o que**   foi   **foi**   é   **é**   passado   **passado**

vira   **vira**   vir   **vir**   a   **a**   ver   **ver**

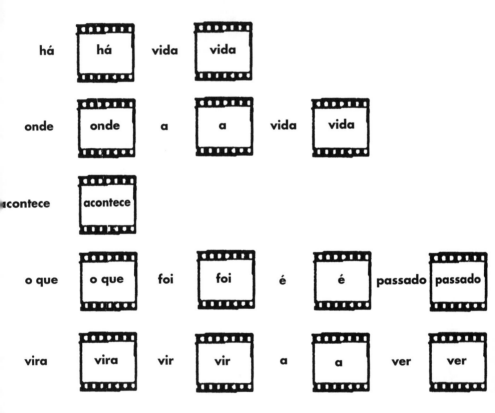

THERE IS THERE IS LIFE LIFE

WHERE WHERE THE THE LIFE LIFE

HAPPENS HAPPENS

WHAT WHAT WAS WAS IS IS PAST PAST

TURNS TURNS WILL COME WILL COME TO TO SEE SEE

Tr. Michael Palmer

HORÁCIO COSTA

VIII
ZONA

Não conte o número. Sem primeira nem última, as ondas do mar. Fragmentos: diante dos palmeirais, um rebanho lentíssimo. Vêm vêm vêm. Calmaria é dos zebus o mascar indefinido. Exegi monumentum aere perennius. Tantalizing.

VIII
ZONE

Don't count the number. No first or last, the waves of the sea. Fragments: before the palm groves, how slow the flock. They come come come. Calm is zebra's indefinite chewing. Exegi monumentum aere perennius. Tantalizing.

Tr. Charles Perrone

XV
BURACO NEGRO

O animal enfurecido engole seus próprios halos. Negra a cor
da luz interna. O quase, sua máscara. Ouvimos seus queixumes
de anjo omnívoro. No quarto, às escuras, penso em meu pai.

XV
BLACK HOLE

The furious animal swallows its own halos. Black the color
 of the inner light. An almost, its mask. We heard its angelic
omnivorous complaints. In the darkness of the room, I think of my father.

Tr. Charles Perrone

XXI

Qual a área que esconde a liberdade de uma linha?
relacionam-se universos do plano ao monte, arfam pulsares pelos
interstícios. Se te aprouver, inscreve tua fractalidade na pele do papel.

XXI

What space can hide the liberty of a line?
From mountains to plains universes relate, pulsars heave and pant
in interstices. If it please thee, inscribe thy fractality on paper's skin.

Tr. Charles Perrone

XLV
A TENTAÇÃO DE SANTO ANTÔNIO

no céu a terceira **Visão** perscruta ornitorrincos monstruosos
no coração cabeça o **V** do e**V**angelho rói a moldura do menino antigo
debaixo de meus pés *the breaking of the Vessels* os ratos absolutos a absol**V**ição

XLV
THE TEMPTATION OF SAINT ANTHONY

in the heavens the third Vision examines monstrous ornithorhyncus
in the head heart the **V** of e**V**angelism gnaws the frame of the ancient boy
under my feet the breaking of the **V**essels the absolute rats absol**V**ing

Tr. Charles Perrone

O RETRATO DE DOM LUIS DE GÔNGORA

cara de vampiro, nariz boxeado pela vida,
stiffness, teu legendário orgulho desmesurado,
sem ironia ou sorriso a boca nos cantos desce,
não vejo tuas mãos, estarão escrevendo,
estarão manipulando o ábaco da sintaxe,
preocupado te vejo em encontrar tesouros
dormentes, na folha branca brilham larvais,
e já fixos me perfuram teus olhos de esfinge,
que imitam tuas orelhas em leque, teu manteau
absoluto, mole de lã ou veludo, sempre Diretor
dum hospital barroco antes do Grand Renfermement,
para quem posas, cantas o Esgueva do pensamento
de teus contemporâneos, o radical suspiro da Natureza
em cio profundo, linguagem láctea, campo blau,
e me avalias, por fora Ácis, por dentro Polifemo.
assim é o mundo Dom Luís, para mim estás posando,
pré-kafkiana barata insigne vai de ante em ante-sala,
paciente expõe seu elástico decoro enfático, tanto
tens que suportar, por fora Hyde, por dentro tão menino,
pois és menino e más allá da moldura deste quadro
como os negros falas—é de noite que em pérola
se transforma a banalidade, e tua calva preenche
o céu, cede o vazio, e tua palavra uma berceuse escapa.

México, 1984

PORTRAIT OF DON LUIS DE GÔNGORA

vampire face, life-battered nose,
stiffness your immoderate pride,
the corners of your smile drawn down without irony,
I do not see your hands, they might be writing,
they might be manipulating syntax's abacus,
I see you absorbed in seeking dormant treasures,
larvae shimmer on the white page,
and your sphinx eyes, now fixed, penetrate me
they imitate your fan-like ears, your full cloak,
a mass of velvet or wool, Director always
of a baroque hospital before the Grand Renfermement,
for whom do you pose? you sing of the Esgueva
of your contemporaries' thought, the radical sigh
of Nature in deep heat, lacteal language, azure field,
and you value me, Acis without, Polyphemus within,
this is the world Don Luis, you are sitting for me,
distinguished pre-Kafkan cockroach goes from ante
to anteroom, patiently expounds his emphatic elastic decorum,
this much you must put up with, Jekyll without,
so small within, because you are child and beyond
the canvas' frame you speak as blacks do—it is at night
that banality becomes a pearl, and your baldness fills the sky,
the void yields, and a lullaby escapes your word.

México, 1984

Tr. Martha Black Jordan

HISTÓRIA NATURAL

Detrás do taxidermista, há a palha,
detrás do rinoceronte, a savana,
detrás desta escritura só a noite,
a noite que galopa até o fronte.

Na asa da mariposa assoma a lua,
na cabeça do alfinete brilha o sol,
nestas linhas reverbera um sol negro,
o astro que ora sobe no horizonte.

O animal dissecado da sintaxe
provê o verbo, o bastidor e a legenda
duma coleção mais morta que os mortos.

No gabinete de história natural
o visitante-leitor detém-se face
a mamíferos e insetos reluzentes.

NATURAL HISTORY

Behind the taxidermist, there's the straw,
behind the rhinoceros, the savannah,
behind this writing only the night,
night which gallops to the fore.

The moon leaps from the butterfly's wing,
the sun shines on the head of a pin,
a black sun thrums through these lines,
star now rising on the horizon.

The dessicated animal of syntax
furnishes the word, the frame and the label
of a collection deader than the dead.

In the natural history collection
the visiting reader pauses alongside
shining mammals and insects.

Tr. Martha Black Jordan
Previously unpublished

CARLOS ÁVILA

O SOL

O sol
(a ser adjetivado:
im-pla-cá-vel)
descorou a capa
de um volume de baudelaire

as flores do mal
(descubro)
não resistem à lenta
violência do sol
(sol de boca-de-sertão
que estorrica o solo?)

também
quem mandou colocar a estante
nesta posição:
o que estaria baudelaire
(em efígie gráfica)
fazendo no sertão?

se as flores do mal
não suportam o sol
(responde baudelaire)
resistiriam aos punhais
do óxido e do sal?

THE SUN

The sun
(awaiting an adjective:
im-pla-ca-ble)
bleached the cover
of a volume of baudelaire

the flowers of evil
(I discover)
cannot resist the sun's
slow violence
(sun of the backlands' mouth
that blasts the land dry?)

besides,
who had the shelf
put there:
what would baudelaire
(in graphic effigy)
be doing in the backlands?

if the flowers of evil
can't stand the sun
(answers baudelaire)
how could they resist the thrusts
of salt and rust?

Tr. Regina Alfarano
Previously unpublished

NARCISSUS POETICUS

secou

(no vaso
 sem água)

mal plantado
numa waste land
(minúscula)
de apartamento sombrio:
como resistir
a pó poeira poluição?

maltratado ex-narciso
à própria sorte abandonado
(rente ao piso)
sem fonte
nem espelho

secou
(só no vaso)
sem suor nem saliva
sem lágrima
que o pudesse salvar

NARCISSUS POETICUS

dried up

(in a waterless
vase)

ill planted
in a (tiny)
waste land
of the dim apartment:
how to resist
dust dirt pollution?

mistreated ex-narcissus
abandoned to its fate
(flat on the floor)
without well
or mirror

dried up
(alone in the vase)
without sweat or saliva
or tears
to save it

morreu
(fuligem
na alma)

died
(soot
on its soul)

Tr. Regina Alfarano
Previously unpublished

RÉGIS BONVICINO

A DESORDEM DE

A desordem de sucessivos

ateliês herdeiros de Picasso

pagaram impostos com desenhos

Derain Cézanne Matisse Seurat

Contra um fundo de azul mútuo

Picasso—mulher com orelha

grande e a cabeça de Fernande

Pábulo de vermes Picasso

colecionava Picuá de barro

decorado com cabra

Picasso cavado com camisa

de listas. Testa olhos nariz

e morena boca de Françoise

Gilot

THE DISORDER OF

The disorder of successive

ateliers Picasso's heirs

paid taxes with drawings

Derain Cézanne Matisse Seurat

Against a backdrop of reciprocal blue

Picasso—woman with large

ear and Fernande's head

Passel of worms Picasso

collected Pitcher of clay

decorated with she-goat

hollowed-out Picasso with striped

shirt. Forehead eyes nose

and olive mouth of Françoise

Gilot

o arco de sobrancelhas marca

os olhos claros (quadris largos)

pétalas de fina fêmeaflor

Em Horta de Ebro Tarragona

Boulevard de Clichy Cadaqués

Picasso e Braque em Céret Eva Gouel

Putas de Aviñón vaso, garrafa

jornais e a cor das letras kou

Boulevard Raspail Stein Sorgues

(e as futuras luas de Eluárd)

Eva morre de tuberculose

Roma Montrouge Olga Koklova

Derain no front e a "Guitarra" sem corda

Picasso propôs um diálogo

entre o espaço e a luz

the arch of eyebrows highlights

the clear eyes (large hips)

petals of slender femaleflower

the Garden of Ebro Tarragona

Boulevard de Clichy Cadaqués

Picasso and Braque in Céret Eva Gouel

Whores of Avignon vase, carafe

newspapers and the color of the letters kou

Boulevard Raspail Stein Sorgues

(and Eluard's future moons)

Eva dies from tuberculosis

Rome Montrouge Olga Koklova

Derain at the front and the stringless "Guitar"

Picasso proposed a dialogue

between space and light

Tr. Michael Palmer

FOLHAS

Folhas fêmeas da mandrágora
mandrágoras do agora quando
abutres habitam
azuis

bocas mais suaves do que
vinho
o sol de janeiro queima
a pele

ouriços trucidam víboras
salamandras e consoantes
sob o musgo
de cifras

(como se diz
não se adia
a cor
da noite)

camaleões
o casco oco de um cervo
lacraias mancas
a cauda de um pavão emérito

LEAVES

Female mandrake leaves
mandrakes of this moment when
vultures inhabit
the blue

mouths softer than
wine
january sun burns
the skin

burs slay vipers
salamanders and consonants
under the moss
of ciphers

(as they say
the color
of night
can't be delayed)

chameleons
hollow hoof of deer
maimed centipedes
tail of an illustrious peacock

Tr. Michael Palmer

NOITE (2)

Noite sem trabalho
de pôr-do-sol. Sem
trabalho de lua
índigo e o vazio

do azul anoitece
trabalho de céu?
sem força de estrelas
confinado espaço

Esforço de cor
os vidros ecoam
trabalho da noite
e só amanhece

NIGHT (2)

Night without sunset's
work without
moon's work
indigo and the blue

empty twilight
sky's place?
without star's force
confined space

Effort of colors
the glasses echo
night's work
and daybreak

Tr. by the author, with revisions by Robert Creeley

QUADRADO

(para Bruna)

Uma formiga
picando nuvens
formigas traçam

trilhas quadradas
enquanto brancas
nuvens passam

o pôr-do-sol
e as girafas
de quatro em quatro

QUADRATE

(to Bruna)

One ant
cropping clouds
ants trace

quadrate paths
while white
clouds pass

the sunset
giraffes
four by four

Tr. by the author, with revisions by Robert Creeley

NÃO NADA

Não nada ainda do outro
semelhante ainda ao mesmo
mínimo ainda o outro
ele mesmo não ainda outro
de um mesmo morto outro
insulado em seu corpo

Vincos do mesmo ainda
no íntimo do outro tampouco
cicatrizes unem
tatuagens dissipam
antenas clavadas, em tinta
cacos do outro estilhaços do outro

Uma borboleta fixa encobre
cicatrizes num corpo

NO NOTHING

No nothing still the other
similar still to the same
minimal still the other
he himself not yet the other
of the same dead another
secluded in his body

Traces still of the same
deep inside the other not yet
scars link
tattoos dissipate
bludgeoned antennas, in ink
shards of the other splinters of the other

A stilled butterfly screens
scars on a body

Tr. Regina Alfarano, revised by Dana Stevens

ME TRANSFORMO

Me transformo
outro janela—
outro
que se afasta e não se reaproxima

nas desobjetivações e reativações,
nas linhas e realinhamentos
outros
me atravessam

morto de ser
coisas perdem sentido
expressões figuradas como
ossos de borboleta

me transformo
na observação
de uma pétala

*

Me destransformo
a mesma janela—
outro
que não se afasta

I TRANSFORM MYSELF

I transform myself,
another window—
another
withdrawing and not returning

in disobjectivations and reactivations,
in lines and realignments
others
traverse me

dead of being
things lose sense
figurative expressions
like butterfly bones

I transform myself
by observing
a petal

*

I untransform myself
the same window—
another
not withdrawing

Nas objetivações
alinhamentos
e linhas inexistentes
iguais me repassam

Retrato desativado
taxidermista de mim mesmo

In objectivations,
inexistent lines
and alignments
alike repassing me

Deactivated portrait,
taxidermist of myself.

Tr. Charles Perrone

ONDE

Onde eu escrevo
há o ruído
do lixo da cidade depois
de recolhido
sendo triturado

há um abajur
uma cômoda
com espelho
e uma cama
desarrumada

o outono está próximo
a janela fechada

um cansaço súbito
toma conta das palavras.

NYC/29 set/1994

WHERE

Where I write
there's the noise
of the city garbage after
it's collected
being ground

there's a lamp
a chest of drawers
with a mirror
and a bed
unmade

autumn is near
the window closed

a sudden fatigue
takes charge of the words.

NYC/Sept 29/1994

Tr. John Milton

SEM TÍTULO

Éden de pétalas secas

Formiga de abdômen inchado

Sombras de figuras idênticas

—Sóis excluídos—

Víboras

Perto de tempos perdidos sóis

que não podem ser identificados

(O carro rói alissos e verbenas)

Pétalas vistas pela janela

Inexistente nuvem que se movimenta

NO TITLE

Eden of dry petals

Ant with swollen abdomen

Shadows of identical figures

—Suns excluded—

Vipers

Near the lost times suns

which cannot be identified

(The car crunches alyssums and verbenas)

Petals seen through the window

A nonexistent cloud that moves

Tr. John Milton

JOSELY VIANNA BAPTISTA

OS POROS FLÓRIDOS

Fim de tarde, as sombras suam
sua tintura sobre as cores, extraem
da fava rara da luz o contorno das coisas,
as rugas na concha de um molusco,
grafismos, vieiras milenares com reservas
de sal, poema estranho trançado
em esgarços de oleandros,
enquanto corpos
mergulham em câmara lenta,
e nada é imagem
(teu corpo branco em mar de sargaços),
nada é miragem
na tela rútila das pálpebras.

FLORID PORES

Late afternoon, the shadows spill
their tints over colors, extract
the contour of things from the light's odd grain,
the grooves on a mollusk shell,
tracings, millenary scallops with salt
deposits, strange poem woven
among shreds of oleander
while bodies
dive in slow motion
and nothing is image
(your white body engulfed in seaweed)
nothing is mirage
on the eyelids' shining screen.

Tr. Michael Palmer
Previously unpublished

UM SOM DE ANTIGAS ÁGUAS APAGADAS.

... miragem a rima, a fábula do nada,
    as falhas dessa fala em desgeografia,
a fala hermafrodita, imantação de astilhas,
a voz na transparência, edifícios de areia.

Mas teu olhar o mesmo, em íris-diafragma,
    fotogramas a menos na edição do livro,
e o enredo sonho e sol, delírios insulares,
    teu olhar transparente, a imagem
margem d'água, e as fábulas da fala,
as falhas desse nada—superfície de alvura

                ou árida escritura.

        Na moldura da página,
        marginália de escarpas.

A SOUND OF ANCIENT, FADED FLOWS

...the rhyme is a mirage, fable of nothingness,
the flaws of speech deterritorialized,
hermaphroditic speech, splinters magnetized,
voice through transparency, buildings of sand.

But your gaze the same, an iris-diaphragm,
   photograms missing from the published book,
the sun and dream plot and insular deliriums,
   your transparent gaze, the image
water's edge, and the fables of speech,
the flaws of such nothingness—a surface of whitness

      or arid scribblings.

At page's border,
marginalia of slopes.

Tr. Michael Palmer
Previously unpublished

INFINITS

para nietzsche

entre bétulas e nadas, nadas
e madrugadas, beats, fadas, f
ugas, árias, entre gélidas p
étalas de neve, leves crista
is limando *nichts* de fumaça
, entre picos e abismos, bét
ulas e nadas, lá, onde o ar
falta: ali sua fala limalha
polindo tudo e um isso: no c
repúsculo dos ídolos, divinos
idos (andarilho entre verd
ades e mentiras), à procura da
flor que brota, rara na rocha,
entre *neins* e pistilos, aurora
, pedra lascada: na a lta
engadina valquírias cav algam
luas que ainda uivam para
lous, e o visionário, no
limiar, parindo centauros

INFINITES

for nietzsche

between birches and nothing
s, nothings and dawns, beat
s, fairies, fugues, arias, am
ong frozen snow petals, lig
ht crystals polishing *nichts*
of smoke, among peaks and
abysses, birches and nothin
gs, there, where there's no
air: there your sandy speech
polishing everything, and a
this: at the sunset of the
idols, once divine (wanderer
among truths and lies)
searching for the blooming
flower, rare on the rock,
among neins and pistils,
aurora, hewn stone: on the
high engadine walkyries
ride on moons that still
howl to lous, and the
visionary, on the threshold,
giving birth to centaurs

Tr. Regina Alfarano

um   dia   eufórica
outros   por   for   a
um   dia   engag   ée
outro   retom   bée
apuro   um   d   ia
outro   rigor   e   o
dia   urzes   e
alcaçuzes   vez   es
que   bruxa   o
utrasque   musa   se
um   dia   blan   co   os
outros   s   alvos
um   dia   d   esfeita
outrosperfeita   um
ou   tro   em   dia   um
d   ia   um   outro   dia
sem   d   nem   você

one day euphoric other
stratospheric one day
engagée another
retombée if plight one
day rigor another and
the day heather and
licorice at times a
witch others a muse if
one day blanco others
saved if one day right
others savaged one up
to date one day
another day with-out
' d ' without thee

Tr. Regina Alfarano

graal em vila velha ou na p
onte vecchio, nas lajes lim
adas pelos grãos de areia, n
a listra riscada entre ped
ra e líquen , arestas de ja
de, cristas de granito, em i
lhas de minas, nebulosidad
es, nas margens tranquila
s que o granizo frisa , nu
m fremir de lábios, retini
r de dentes , na tua alegri
a ou no senso em deslize d
os olhos em falso descobr
indo ocelos nas asas estria
das de um pequeno
inseto

grail   at   vila   velha   or   ponte
vecchio,   on   slabs   sanded   by
tiny   sand   grains,in   the   ledge   d
rawn   between   the   rock   and
lichens,   and   jade   edges,   granite
crests,in   island   mines,   neb
ulosities,   on   the   tranquil
margins   which   hail   crisps   ,   in
the   quivering   of   lips,   ringing   of
teeth,   in   your   happiness   or   in
the   sliding   sense   of   misled   eyes
sighting   ocelli   in   the   f   luted
wings   of   a   little   insect

Tr. Regina Alfarano

na madrugada fria a pai
sagem se vê através da p
aisagem, a geada e a lasc
a de um jaspe que se par
ece ao jade, as gazes da g
eada que esfumam a pais
agem, e a lasca de um j
aspe que se parece ao ja
de e se repete jaspe na
geada paisagem, na casc
a de áspide , na valsa
de uma vespa, no rasgo
de um outdoor, na aura d
e um poema, na mineral f
umaça da boca de quem
fala, no ar em ar *a*
r s que condensa uma im
agem, geada, jade, jaspe n
a pele da paisagem, q ue
o áspero da espera alter a
em miragem: formigas t
raçam trilhas na farinha

in cold dawn, landscape is seen
through other landscape, white frost
and jasper sliver that looks like
jade, with frost gauzes shading the
hazy landscape , and the jasper sliver
that looks like jade and repeats
itself in the frost landscape, in the
skin of an asp , in the waltz of a
wasp ,in the slit of a billboard , in
the aura of a poem, in the mineral
smoke from one whispering mouth , in
the air in to air into *ars* that
condense an image, white frost, and
geode, and jade , and jasper on the
face of this landscape, and changed
into a mirage by asperities of
waiting:some ants are tracing tracks
in flour

Tr. Regina Alfarano

NELSON ASCHER

ONDE HÁ FUMAÇA

dann steigt ihr als Rauch in die Luft
PAUL CELAN

Fumaça alguma implica
memória, já que as coisas
se perdem na fumaça
que, assim, tampouco pode

tornar-se um monumento,
pois sendo transitória
nem mesmo homenageia
a transitoriedade.

Fumaça enquanto tinta,
embora branca (um branco
mais palidez de horror
qua alvura de inocência),

serve talvez à escrita;
porém, não há destreza
que inscreva na fumaça,
como na pedra, um nome.

Quando a fumaça, quase
vegetativa, irrompe e,
traindo o genealógico,
assume aspecto arbóreo,

WHERE THERE'S SMOKE

dann steigt ihr als Rauch in die Luft
PAUL CELAN

No smoke implies
memory, since things
are lost in smoke
which cannot thus

become a monument,
for being transitory, it
pays no homage
even to transitoriness.

Smoke as ink,
though white (a white more
of horror's pallor
than purity's innocence),

may serve for writing;
but where's the skill
that inscribes a name,
in smoke, as in a rock?

When smoke, near-
vegetal, erupts and,
betraying genealogy,
takes on arboreal shape,

não cabe perguntar
acerca (onde há fumaça,
há cinzas) das raízes
mais fundas da fumaça.

one mustn't ask
about (where there's smoke,
there's ash) the deepest
roots of smoke.

Tr. Dana Stevens

AMOR

O olhar desapropria
a forma alheia, o ouvido
sequestra a voz alheia,
o olfato rapta o odor

alheio, o paladar
rouba o sabor alheio,
o tato furta a carne
alheia, ou seja, a própria;

reluz o olhar alheio
do visto em outro, ecoa
o ouvido alheio um outro,
rescende o olfato alheio

a um outro, sabe a um outro
o paladar alheio,
tateia o tato alheio
um outro, ou seja, o mesmo.

LOVE

Sight dispossesses
the form of the other, hearing
sequesters the voice of the other,
smell abducts the odor

of the other, taste
steals the flavor of the other,
touch snatches the flesh
of the other, that is, one's own;

the look of the other gleams
from what is seen in another,
the ear of the other echoes another,
the scent of the other rises

to another, the flavor of the other
tastes of another
the other touch palpates another
that is, the very same.

Tr. Regina Alfarano

MÁQUINAS

Se—máquinas precisas
que somos de morrer—
nossa função implica
memória
ininterrupta,

por que, afinal, possuis
(lubrificadamente
contrátil entre as pernas)
o teu lagar de amnésia?

MACHINES

If—precise machines
for dying that we are—
our function implies
unending memory,

why, then, do you bear
(lubriciously
contractile between your legs)
your wine-press of amnesia?

Tr. Regina Alfarano

FLAGRANTE

Opaco, mas translúcido
durante o ocaso, como
pomar onde a ramagem
das árvores frutíferas

admite obliquamente
a luz emaranhada,
o *nylon* do vestido
que vestes filtra o sol

exangue, cujos raios,
a fim de desenhar-te,
imbricam-se num último
flagrante, que dirime

a sede da retina
na qual se imprime (nítida
radiografia) o teu
contorno curvilíneo.

SNAPSHOT

Opaque, but translucent
at sunset, like
an orchard where branches
of bearing trees

obliquely admit
the tangled light,
the nylon of the dress
you wear filters the

bloodless sun, whose rays,
in their attempt to draw you,
betray themselves in a final
snapshot appeasing

the retina's thirst
to imprint there (vivid
x-ray) your
curving shape.

Tr. Regina Alfarano

BASHÔ EM PARIS

para Rose

Manhã de gala:
flores, imóveis
damas desnudas,
desfilam cores.

Midi le juste:
suicida , o sol,
no mar de suor,
se põe a pino.

Tarde-alfarrábio:
folhas em verde,
como as impressas,
amarelescem.

Que noite albina!
A torre, embora
de ferro, quase
treme de frio.

BASHO IN PARIS

for Rose

Gala morning:
flowers, motionless
naked ladies,
parade colors.

Midi le juste:
suicidal, the sun,
in a sea of sweat,
sets at high noon.

Second-hand afternoon:
leaves of green,
like printed sheets,
turn yellow.

Albino night!
The tower, though
iron, almost
shivers from cold.

Tr. Regina Alfarano

MEU CORAÇÃO

Mein Herz, mein Herz ist träurig

HEINE

Se tenho um coração maior que
o mundo, por que seus ventrículos
fecham-se em pontos tão ridículos
quando oxigênio algum retorque

as carências da carne? à parte
isso, o lipídio sujo encarde o
sangue que irriga o miocárdio
por dentro até que o seu enfarte

maciço torne enfim as várias
figuras líricas, diletas—
letais. Dizei-me, enfim , poetas:
o amor entope as coronárias?

MY HEART

Mein Herz, mein Herz ist träurig
HEINE

If my heart is larger than
the world, why then do these ventricles
close down into ridiculous points
when no oxygen at all replies

to the needs of the flesh? What's more,
the dense lipid stains
the blood that floods the myocardium
internally until a massive

stroke finally turns the various
lyric figures, so esteemed—
lethal. Then, poets, do tell me:
can love clog the coronaries?

Tr. Regina Alfarano

AGE DE CARVALHO

PASSAGEM

Era julho
floresciam pedras
carregavas a sombra de um rio

Chamavam-nos
agosto, norte, ninguém

Irreconciliáveis

PASSAGE

It was July
stones were blooming
you hauled the river's shadow

We were called:
august, north, nobody

Irreconcilable.

Tr. Dana Stevens

NEGATIVO DE RICARDO REIS

Bocas roxas (não
de vinho),
sobre a testa
branca cresce a erva

Não te chamo Lídia : nada
sabemos sobre o rio das coisas

NEGATIVE OF RICARDO REIS

Mouths purple (not
with wine),
above the white
brow grass grows

I don't call you Lydia: we know
nothing of the river of things

Tr. Dana Stevens

A IDADE DO CARVALHO

A idade do carvalho
aflora real na pedra
(ágrafo círculo da pedra,
a sombra e a diferença)
aponta para o deserto,
declina
       o ramo do nome
onde espera uma data,
a resposta

THE AGE OF THE OAK

The age of the oak
blossoms from stone
(unwritten circle of stone,
shadow and difference)
points to the desert,
inflects
      the branch of a name,
awaits a date,
the answer

Translated by the author

a Monika Grond

A CURA, e a sua aura
esvaziada de abismo

O abismo—o íntimo
      ascender

um estrelar-se infinito
      (de boca
contra) ao beijo cru
da queda

for Monika Grond

The CURE, and its emptied
air of abyss

The abyss—the intimate
       ascending

an infinite starring
       (of mouth
against) the raw kiss
of falling

Tr. Dana Stevens

ANGELA DE CAMPOS

A corcova calva do camelo
me traz o desejo
de incendiar as vogais
e ruminar as cinzas arenosas.

Como a alma acalma o coração?
Talvez com dromedários.

The camel's bald hump
wakes my desire
to burn the vowels
and chew the gritty ashes.

How does the soul soothe the heart?
Maybe with dromedaries.

Tr. Michael Palmer

A tarde se estira
no dorso de um tigre
veloz—
o duro mel dos olhos
encorpa em camélias
súbitas esquinas sem beijos,—
todos os minutos se espreitam.

Afternoon stretches out
on the back of a swift
tiger—
the hard honey of the eyes
thickens into camellias
sudden corners without kisses,—
all the minutes spy on each other.

Tr. Michael Palmer

O tempo soluça no relógio
as rugas horizontais
que não tatuam meu rosto.
Ponteiros
agulhas invisíveis
injetam o ritmo
que infecta o dia.

Time hiccups from the clock
the horizontal wrinkles
that don't tattoo my face
Invisible needles
its hands
inject the rhythm
that infects the day

Tr. Michael Palmer

ARNALDO ANTUNES

algo é o nome do homem
coisa é o nome do homem
homem é o nome do cara
isso é o nome da coisa
cara é o nome do rosto
fome é o nome do moço
homem é o nome do troço
osso é o nome do fóssil
corpo é o nome do morto
homem é o nome do outro

something is the man's name
thing is the man's name
man is the guy's name
this is the thing's name
face is the head's name
hunger is the boy's name
man is the stuff's name
bone is the fossil's name
body is the dead's name
man is the other's name

Tr. Dana Stevens

As   coisas   têm   peso,
massa,   volume,   tamanho,
tempo, forma, cor, posição,
textura,   duração,
densidade,   cheiro,
valor, consistência,   pro-
fundidade,   contorno,
temperatura,   função,
aparência, preço, destino,
idade,   sentido.   As   coisas
não têm paz.

Things   have   weight,
mass,   volume,   size,
time,   form,   color,
position, texture, dura-
tion,   density,   smell,
worth,   consistency,
depth, contour, temper-
ature, function, appear-
ance, price, destiny, age,
meaning. Things have no
peace.

Tr. Regina Alfarano and Dana Stevens

As pedras são muito mais lentas do que os animais. As plantas exalam mais cheiro quando a chuva cai. As andorinhas quando chega o inverno voam até o verão. Os pombos gostam de milho e de migalhas de pão. As chuvas vêm da água que o sol evapora. Os homens quando vêm de longe trazem malas. Os peixes quando nadam juntos formam um cardume. As larvas viram borboletas dentro dos casulos . Os dedos dos pés evitam que se caia. Os sábios ficam em silêncio quando os outros falam. As máquinas de fazer nada não estão quebradas. Os rabos dos macacos servem como braços. Os rabos dos cachorros servem como risos. As vacas comem duas vezes a mesma comida. As páginas foram escritas para serem lidas. As árvores podem viver mais tempo que as pessoas. Os elefantes e golfinhos têm boa memória. Palavras podem ser usadas de muitas maneiras. Os fósforos só podem ser usados uma vez. Os vidros quando estão bem limpos quase não se vê. Chicletes são pra mastigar mas não para engolir. Os dromedários têm uma corcova e os camelos têm duas. As meia-noites duram menos do que os meio-dias. As tartarugas nascem em ovos mas não são aves. As baleias vivem na água mas não são peixes. Os dentes quando a gente escova ficam brancos. Cabelos quando ficam velhos ficam brancos. As músicas dos índios fazem cair chuva. Os corpos dos mortos enterrados adubam a terra. Os carros fazem muitas curvas pra subir a serra. Crianças gostam de fazer perguntas sobre tudo. Nem todas as respostas cabem num adulto.

Stones are much slower than animals. Plants give off more scent when it rains. Swallows fly south for the winter. Doves like corn and breadcrumbs. Rain comes from water that the sun evaporates. When men come from far off, they bring suitcases. Fish swimming together form a school. Caterpillars become butterflies in their cocoons. Toes keep you from falling. Wise men are quiet when others speak. Machines for doing nothing are not broken. Monkeys' tails are used as arms. Dogs' tails are used as smiles. Cows eat the same food twice. Pages are written to be read. Trees live longer than people. Elephants and dolphins have good memories. Words can be used in many ways. Matches can only be used once. When glass is clean you can hardly see it. Gum is to chew but not to swallow. Dromedaries have one hump and camels have two. Midnights are shorter than middays. Turtles hatch from eggs but aren't birds. Whales live in water but aren't fish. Teeth turn white when you brush them. Hair turns white when it gets old. The songs of Indians make rain fall. Buried bodies of the dead fertilize the earth. Cars make many curves to climb a mountain. Children like to ask questions about everything. Not all the answers fit in an adult.

Tr. Regina Alfarano and Dana Stevens

QUASE

agagueiraquasepalavra
quaseaborta
apalavraquasesilêncio
quasetransborda
osilêncioquaseeco

ALMOST

thestammeralmostword
almostaborts
thewordalmostsilence
almostoverflows
thesilencealmostecho

Tr. Regina Alfarano and Dana Stevens
Previously unpublished

QUE NÃO É O QUE NÃO PODE SER

poema musicado

poem set to music

Tr. Dana Stevens

CARLITO AZEVEDO

OURO PRETO

Anjo não, *Anjo*:
como se um sopro
lhe sobre as asas
batesse e quase

voasse e caso
voasse sendo
leveza menos
que exatidão.

Anjo de igreja
ao ar aberto
(a nave: a nuvem?)

sabeis a pedra-
sabão, a melhor,
a bolha-de-.

OURO PRETO

Not an angel, an *Angel*:
as if a breeze
beat over his wings
and nearly

flew and if it
flew was less
lightness
than precision.

Church angel
in open air
(boat: cloud?)

you taste of soap-
stone, the best,
the bubble of.

Tr. Dana Stevens

BANHISTA

Apenas
        em frente
ao mar
        um dia de verão—
quando tua voz
            acesa percorresse,
consumindo-o,
            o pavio de um verso
até sua última
            sílaba inflamável—
quando o súbito
            atrito de um nome
em tua memória te
            incendiasse os cabelos—
(e sobre tua pele
            de fogo a
brisa fizesse
        rasgaduras
de água)

BATHER

Barely
             before
the sea
             one summer's day—
when your voice,
             lit, traversed,
consuming it,
             the wick of a poem
until its last
             tindered syllable—
when the sudden
             friction of a name
in your memory
             set your hair ablaze—
(and on your skin
             of fire a
breeze ripped
             like water)

Tr. Dana Stevens

NA NOITE GRIS

Na noite gris
este fulgor
no ar? Tigres

à espreita? Claro
sol de um cigarro
em lábios-lis?

Na lixa abrupta
súbita chispa?
Choque de peles

a contra-pelo
(tal numa rua
escura mutua-

mente se enlaçam
as contra-luzes
de dois faróis)?

IN GREY NIGHT

In grey night
this luster
in air? Tigers

lurking? Pale
sun of a cigarette
at lily-lips?

In sandpaper's roughness
a sudden glare?
The shock of skins

against hair
(as in a dark
street doub-

ly enlace
the counterbeams
of two headlights)?

Tr. Dana Stevens

A MARGARIDA-PÉROLA

Severo e estranho rumo
conduz-nos ao mais puro
prazer: roçar a pétala
da margarida-pérola,
luzente, eletrizando-se
no atrito entanto doce;
fazer vergar num átimo
de tempo, ao fogo, o sândalo
que a nada então reduz-se,
silente, à ação da luz e
calor. Exala o cheiro-
madeleine de um chiqueiro,
no pratos o porco, istmo
de podre e preciosismo.

PEARL-DAISY

Severe and strange course
leads us to the purest
pleasure: to graze the petal
of the pearl-daisy
shining, self-electrifying
in the gentle friction;
to make it bend in
a nanosecond, the sandalwood then,
in the fire, shrinks to nothing,
silent under the force of heat
and light. It exhales the *madeleine-*
scent of a pigsty,
pig on the plate, strait
of preciosity and rot.

Tr. Michael Palmer

RELENDO *SAXÍFRAGA*

A flor de luz febril
do gozo medra em misto
de covardia e brio.

Mas mina o corpo (a rocha
do corpo) e logo em fúria
e em fogo desabrocha.

Quer ir além do corpo?
por onde aéreas pétalas
de nada ou de torpor?

O olhar pára, decifra
(garança entre vermelhos)
um perfume em *Saxífraga*.

REREADING *SAXIFRAGE*

The febrile light-flower
of desire swells into a mix
of courage and cowardice.

But it undermines the body (the rock
of the body) and soon it blooms
in fury and fire.

Wants to transcend the body?
toward aerial petals
of stupor and emptiness?

The gaze halts, deciphers
(rose-madder among reds)
a scent in *Saxifrage.*

Tr. Michael Palmer

FREDERICO BARBOSA

LASCAUX 1986

no cinema de Lascaux
(imagem sobre imagem)
cortes:
séculos de Klee

recortes de cores
nos desenhos do Kane
na voz bellae
(Billie & Ella)
nas suas pernas cruzadas
em frente à tv

mágico quase acaso
colorindo
(como que sem querer)
a caverna escura
em que a gente se vê

LASCAUX 1986

at the Cinema Lascaux
(image over image)
cuts:
centuries of Klee

cross-sections of colors
in the drawings of Kane
in the bellae voice
(Billie & Ella)
in her crossed legs
in front of the TV

chance-like magic
coloring
as if by accident
the dark cavern
in which we find ourselves

Tr. Michael Palmer

RAREFATO

Nenhuma voz humana aqui se pronuncia
chove um fantasma anárquico,   demolidor

amplo nada no vazio deste deserto
anuncia-se como ausência,   carne em unha

     odor silencioso no vento   escarpa
corte de um espectro   pousando   na água

tudo que escoa em silêncio em tempo ecoa

RAREFACTUS

No human voice   here   speaks out
an anarchic phantom pours,   demolisher

full nothing in the emptiness of this desert
offers itself as absence,   nail flesh

     silent scent in the wind   slope
spectre's cross-section   at rest   in the water

all that in silence flows in due time echoes

Tr. Michael Palmer

RUY VASCONCELOS DE CARVALHO

PIANO

sob o jasmineiro
em flor, um passante

recolhe uma moeda
no instante em que

o velho, com um
quarto minguante de

dedos, quebra o
chapéu sobre a testa

PIANO

beneath the flowering
jasmine, a passerby

retrieves a coin
that same instant when

the old man, with the
quarter moon of his

fingers, pulls his hat
low on his forehead

Tr. Michael Palmer
Previously unpublished

CLÓVIS BEVILÁQUA NO DIA DOS NAMORADOS

hoje ao cruzar a praça
clóvis beviláqua me
pareceu especialmente
triste. trazia a cabeça
levemente curvada
para esquerda. debaixo
da axila tratados
jurídicos pesavam sem
desodorante anos à fio
nenhum pardal poderia
penetrar pelas lapelas.
três meninos revezavam
o comando de uma arraia
que repontava sobre a
igreja batista. clóvis
beviláqua sem par, com
bigode de bronze no
meio da praça. deixei-o
com a notável solidão
saber jurídico, reputação
que desconheço, mas
desconsolo mais notório
no dia dos namorados.

CLÓVIS BEVILÁQUA ON VALENTINE'S DAY

today as I crossed the square
clóvis beviláqua seemed
particularly sad
his head bent
slightly to the left.
beneath his arm
legal tracts have hung
odoriferous these
many years—no sparrow
will penetrate his lapels.
three kids took turns
guiding a kite
which looped above
the baptist church. clóvis
beviláqua all alone, with
moustache of bronze in
the middle of the
square. I left him
to his famous solitude,
judicial knowledge, reputation
I know nothing of, yet despondency
even more evident
on valentine's day.

Tr. Michael Palmer
Previously unpublished

CLAUDIA ROQUETTE-PINTO

MINIMA MORALIA

só a pétala mais rara
carna—
dura estriada
sem transparência de luz
só a pétala folheada
de água
onde mora (aguarda)
o som de uma floresta
pulsação dos fluidos da floresta
quando o tímpano estala

MINIMA MORALIA

only the rarest petal
stri—
ated flesh
devoid of light's transparency
only the water-flecked
petal
wherein dwells (awaits)
the sound of a forest
the throbbing of a forest's fluids
when the eardrum crackles

Tr. Michael Palmer

CASTANHAS, MULHERES

se abertas
com a destra surpresa
de pequenas mãos
cegas a tal alfabeto
e a nesga—já marron—
de pele fere
mais que a tolice dos espinhos
vê como
o gomo lateja:
ela e ela
desabotoa
entre os dedos

CHESTNUTS, WOMEN

if opened
with the surprising skill
of small hands
blind to such an alphabet
and if— itself brown—
the patch of skin bruises
even more than from foolish thorns
see how
the bud throbs:
she and she
unbuttons
between the fingers

Tr. Michael Palmer

RETRATO DE PABLO, VELHO

da sombra seu rosto se lança
um peixe
uma lua africana
boiando à superfície gasta e gris
a calva não dava um aviso
dos olhos vivos
de água, vivos
que engendram antes de ver
a testa de touro tem brio
empurra um nariz repartido:
uma face enfrenta,
a outra subtrai
o resto são rugas e ricto
papiro
e o som de cascos ancestrais

PORTRAIT OF PABLO, AGÈD

from the shadow his face hurls itself forth
a fish
an african moon
floating above the worn and grey surface
the bald spot gave no hint
of the eyes lively
as water, so lively
they create before seeing
the prideful bull's brow
thrusts a split nose:
one side of the face confronts
the other withdraws
the rest is wrinkles and grimace
papyrus
and the sound of ancestral hooves

Tr. Michael Palmer

VÃO

palavra como persiana
poema como lucidez
imanta o ar fora do cômodo
das frases   um outono
rente à janela
ouro tonto sobre a tarde derrubada
entrementes, entre dentes
(e quatro paredes)
tua boca ainda invoca
equívoca e pobre.
na penugem além da vidraça
os deuses-de-tudo-o-que-importa
cerram as pálpebras de cobre

IN VAIN

word like window blind
poem like lucidity
magnetizes the air outside the room
of phrases   autumn
near the pane
dizzy gold over demolished afternoon
between minutes, between teeth,
(and four walls)
your mouth still summoning
equivocal and faint.
in the shutter beyond the glass
the gods-of-everything-that-matters
close copper eyelids

Tr. Michael Palmer
Previously unpublished

CONTRIBUTORS' NOTES

TORQUATO NETO

Torquato Neto was born in Teresina, Piaui, in 1944. In 1972 he committed suicide in Rio de Janeiro. One of the founders of the Tropicalist movement with Caetano Veloso and Gilberto Gil, Neto wrote the lyrics for "Geléia Geral" one of the key songs of the movement. His activities also included directing and acting in underground films. He co-edited the vanguard poetry journal *Navilouca* (1972). In the early 70s he wrote a column for the newspaper *Ultima Hora*, in Rio de Janeiro. His only posthumous book, *Os últimos dias de paupéria*, was edited by Waly Salomão.

ANA CRISTINA CÉSAR

Born in 1952, in Rio de Janeiro, César wrote for newspapers and alternative journals in the 70s. Her published books include: *Cenas de Abril, Correspondência Completa, Luvas de Pelica*—later collected under the title *A teus pés* (Brasiliense, 1982). She was also active in journalism, television and literary research. Her manuscripts were published posthumously under the titles *Escritos da Inglaterra* (Brasiliense, 1985). Her posthumous work also includes the poetry book *Inéditos e Dispersos* (Brasiliense, 1985). On October 29, 1983, César committed suicide.

PAULO LEMINSKI

Born in Curitiba, on August 24, 1945, Leminski led a marginal life, with temporary work in advertising and intermittent collaboration with newspapers and journals. Leminski died on June 6, 1989, from alcohol abuse. His prose publications are: *Catatau*

(1975), *Agora é que são elas* (1986), *Metamorfose* (Iluminuras, 1994) (posthumous). His poetry includes the following publications: *Quarenta Cliques em Curitiba* (1979), *Polonaise* (1980) *Caprichos e Relaxos* (1983), *Distraídos Venceremos* (1987), *La vie en close* (1991) (posthumous). Critical works include: *Basho* (1983), *Leon Trotski, a paixão segundo a revolução* (1986), *Cruz e Souza* (1983), *Anseios críticos* (1986).

F R A N C I S C O   A L V I M

Alvim was born in Araxá, Minas Gerais state, in 1938, and grew up in the area between Rio de Janeiro and Belo Horizonte. After his first book was published—*Sol dos cegos* (1968)—he traveled to Paris, where he lived between 1969 and 1971. After returning to Brazil, he published *Passatempo* (1974) in the pioneering marginal collection "Frenesi." In 1981, Brasiliense Publishing House collected nearly all his work in one volume. *Poesias Reunidas* (1968–1988) and *Claro Enigma* were published in 1988. A diplomat, Alvim currently resides in Barcelona, Spain.

D U D A   M A C H A D O

Born in Salvador, Bahia, in 1944. A major in Social Sciences, he wrote popular music lyrics for the early Tropicalist movement. While living in Rio in the 70s Machado edited the avant-garde poetry review *Pólen*. Later, he moved to São Paulo, where he published the magazines *Zil* (1977) and *Crescente* (1990). He has a PhD in Literature from the University of São Paulo, and makes his living from professional translation work. He has translated Gustave Flaubert, John Ashbery and Allen Ginsberg.

WALY SALOMÃO

Born in Jequié, Bahia, in 1944. He graduated from Law School but never worked as an attorney. A poet, a lyricist, and a promoter of cultural events, Salomão has lived in Rio de Janeiro for many years. His publications include: *Me segura qu'eu vou dar um troço* (prose, 1972), *Gigolô de bibelôs* (prose and poetry—1983), and *Armarinho de Miudezas* (criticism, prose and poetry—1993). With Torquato Neto, he edited the single-issue journal *Navilouca* (1971–74). Salomão has written lyrics for several musicians, among them Caetano Veloso, Jards Macalé and João Bosco. He is one of the permanent curators for the collections of Brazilian artist Hélio Oiticica. His most recent book is entitled *Algaravias/Câmara de Ecos* (Editora 34, 1996).

JÚLIO CASTAÑON GUIMARÃES

Born in 1951. His publications include poetry books: *Vertentes* (1975), *17 peças* (1983), and *Inscrições* (1992); an essay, *Territórios/conjunções: poesias e prosa críticas de Murilo Mendes* (1993). Among others he has translated Francis Ponge, Gertrude Stein, Roland Barthes, George Steiner, Mallarmé, Valéry and Michel Butor. He was the editor for the critical edition of *Crônica da casa assassinada*, by Lucio Cardoso (1991), and the co-editor for the critical edition of *A cinza das horas, Carnaval* and *O ritmo dissoluto*, by Manuel Bandeira (1994). Currently working as a researcher at Casa Rui Barbosa, in Rio de Janeiro.

LENORA DE BARROS

Born on November 6, 1953 in São Paulo. Her first book was *Onde se vê* (1983). Since 1975, Barros has contributed visual poems both to Brazilian and international publications (*Qorpo, Estranho, Flue, Poliester*). In 1984 she participated in the xviith

Bienal de São Paulo, with videotext visual poems. She also participated in the Muestra Internacional de Libros de Artista (Argentina). Her first individual exhibit was in Italy, a collection of work from 1975 to 1990. Barros has curated many exhibits, both at home and abroad. She contributed CD-ROM interactive poems to the *Arte Cidade* (São Paulo). She has translated Octavio Paz (El Mono Gramático) and is currently preparing a book: *Nada haver.*

HORÁCIO COSTA

Born in São Paulo, Brazil, in 1954, pursued his studies in Brazil and in the United States. He has a BA degree from the University of São Paulo (1978), an MA from New York University (1983) and a PhD from Yale University (1994). Costa lives in Mexico City at the moment where he is a professor at UNAM (National Autonomous University of Mexico). Published poetry books include: *28 poemas 6 contos* (1981), *Satori* (1989), *O livro dos fracta* (1990), *The very short stories* (1991), *Los jardines y los poetas* (a bilingual Spanish Portuguese anthology, 1993), *O menino e o travesseiro* (1994). His latest book, *Quadragésimo,* was published in 1996. In addition to extensive critical writing, Costa has translated the poetry of authors such as Elizabeth Bishop and Octavio Paz. He is also an active militant for the rights of homosexuals.

CARLOS ÁVILA

Born in Belo Horizonte, Minas Gerais, in 1955. A poet and a journalist, he edited and participated in several marginal avant-garde journals. His poetry publications include the books *Aqui & Agora* (1981) and *Sinal de Menos* (1989). He is currently preparing a new book, *Asperos,* and publishing essays and poems in journals and newspapers both in Brazil and overseas.

Régis Bonvincino

Born in São Paulo in 1955, where he has lived ever since. In the 70s and 80s he was the editor for several poetry journals: *Poesia em Greve* (1975), *Qorpo Estranho* (1976–1982) and *Muda* (1977). He has participated in many poetry readings outside Brazil. Bonvicino is currently a critic for *Folha de S. Paulo,* a daily newspaper. His poetry books include: *Bicho Papel* (1975), *Régis Hotel* (1978), *Sósia da Cópia* (1983), *Más Companhias* (1987), *33 Poemas* (1990), *Outros poemas* (1993). Children's poetry: *Num zoológico de letras* (1994). Translations: *Litanias de Lua,* poems by Jules LaForgue (1989) and *A Pupila do zero, En la masmédula* (poems by Argentine poet Oliverio Girondo), *Poemas* (poems by Robert Creeley—forthcoming). Critical works: *Desbragada*; organizer of a critical anthology on Edward Braga, *Uma carta uma brasa através,* dialogues with Paulo Leminski (1992). Graduated from Law School in 1978, but never worked as an attorney. Bonvicino earned his living exclusively from poetry in the period between 1979 and 1982. Bonvincino's most recent book is entitled *Ossos de Borboleta* (Editora 34, 1996). He also published *Passagens* this year, translated from the poetry of Michael Palmer. He is preparing a book of essays on Brazilian and International contemporary poetry, *Alguma Crítica.* Bonvicino is, furthermore, the editor of Brazilian poetry for *Serta,* a journal published in Madrid, Spain, by Antonio Domingues Rey for Universidad Nacional de Educación a Distancia.

Josely Vianna Baptista

Born in Curitiba, in 1957. As a poet she has published *AR* (1991) and *Corpografia* (1992). She began translating in 1985, with the work of Alejo Carpentier. She has since translated works by Cabrera Infante, J. Cortázar, Severo Sarduy, Simon Bolívar, Fray

Bartolome de las Casas, Alvaro Mutis, M.Vargas Llosa, Luis Goytisolo, the anthology *Caribe Transplantino: poesia neobarroca cubana e rioplantense* and *Lame,* a collection of poems by Nestor Perlonguer, José Lezama Lima's *Paradiso* (a novel), Fugados (stories) and *A dignidade da Poesia* (essays). With visual artist Francisco Faria, Josely Vianna created a visual-poetic installation for the 5th Biennal in Havana (1994). Currently developing the editorial and translation work for the first three volumes of the collection "Cadernos da Amerindia," with Luli Miranda. The work covers aspects of the culture of South American indigenous groups Mbya-Guarani and Nivacle.

NELSON ASCHER

Born in São Paulo in 1958. He majored in Business Administration at Fundação Getúlio Vargas, but never worked in that field. A literary critic for *Folha de S. Paulo* since 1984, he was the founder and editor of *Revista da USP* from 1988 to 1994. His poetry books include: *Ponta da Lingua* (1983) and *Sonho da Razão* (1993). His translations include *Vida sem fim,* by Lawrence Ferlinghetti, in collaboration with Paulo Leminski (1984), *Folhetim: poemas traduzidos* (1987), *Canção antes da ceifa—poesia húngara moderna* (1990) and *Quase uma elegia* (Editora Sette Letras, 1995), a selection of Joseph Brodsky's poetry. *Poesias e cercanias* (forthcoming) brings together fifteen years of contemporary Brazilian poetry criticism. His most recent poetry book is *Algo de Sol* (Editora 34, 1996). He has also published a volume of political and polemical essays mainly about Central and Eastern Europe, dealing with the fall of communism, the Yugoslav civil war, German reunification and the Holocaust: *Pomos da Discórdia* (Editora 34, 1996). Two collections of his poetry translations are to be published this year (1997), *Tristia,* a selection of Russian poets ranging from Pushkin to the contemporaries, and *Colóquio de Ventríloquos,* with poems translated from the English (Yeats, Eliot, Bishop, Ashbery, Basil Bunting, Cid Corman, Waldrop, Simic, etc.) and other languages. Aided by a Vitae scholarship, he is now working on the translation into Portuguese of a large anthology of modern Hungarian poetry.

AGE DE CARVALHO

Born in Belém, Pará state, in 1958. Majored in architecture and is now a graphic designer by profession. He published *Arquitetura dos ossos* (1980), *A fala entre parênteses* (1982), *Arena, areia* (1986) and *Ror* (1990). He currently lives in Vienna, Austria.

ARNALDO ANTUNES

Born in São Paulo, in 1960. He did not complete his degree in literature at the University of São Paulo. Antunes has edited several poetry magazines: *Almanak 80* (1980), *Kataloki* (1981), and *Atlas* (1988). His published books are *Ou E,* a book of visual poems (1983), *Psia* (1986, 2nd edition, 1991), *Tudos* (1990, currently in its 3rd edition) and *As Coisas* (1992, currently 3rd edition and recipient of Jabuti poetry prize). A musician and a visual artist, Antunes participated in several exhibitions of visual poetry both in Brazil and abroad, during the period from 1983 to 1994. He put together the rock group Titãs with which he released several albums between 1982 and 1992. In 1993, *Nome* (video, book, and CD) was released—a multimedia project including poetry, music and computer animation in partnership with Celia Catunda, Kiko Mistrorigo and Zaba Moreau. It was exhibited at shows and festivals worldwide and received honors at the First Annual New York Video Festival. As a musician, he has released a number of recordings in recent years.

ANGELA DE CAMPOS

Born in Rio de Janeiro, on January 1st, 1960. She completed her courses in literarary studies at the Federal University of Rio de Janeiro (AFRJ) and at the Catholic University of Rio de Janeiro (PUC). Married to a diplomat, she has lived in several cities, among them Mexico City. Her first book, *Feixe de Lontras* (Sete Letras) was published in 1996.

CARLITO AZEVEDO

Born in Rio, in 1961, where he currently lives. His published works are: *Collapsus Linguae* (1991—recipient of Jabuti poetry prize) and *Bathers* (1993). His translations of poetry and prose include Max Jacob, René Char, and Jean Follain. Azevedo earns his living as a poet. He is the director of the Circle of Poetic Research in Rio de Janeiro.

FREDERICO TAVARES BASTOS BARBOSA

Born in Recife, Pernambuco, on February 20, 1961, moving to São Paulo when he was 6. Barbosa began undergraduate studies in Physics and Greek, which he never concluded, though he did major in Portuguese Language and Literature. Faithful to his drop-out philosophy, he never completed his master's program. A literary critic at *Jornal da Tarde* and *Folha de S. Paulo* for some time, he currently teaches Brazilian and Portuguese literature courses. His poems have been published in various journals in Brazil. *Rarefato* (Iluminuras, 1990) and *Nada Feito Nada* (Perspectiva, 1993).

RUY VASCONCELOS DE CARVALHO

Born on March 3, 1963, in Ceará's hinterland. Having moved early to Fortaleze, and later majored in History, Carvalho taught

History and English at the elementary school. In 1991 he finished his Master's program, and presented his thesis "Words in the wind: the moving villages" on oral testimonies collected from Northwestern Ceará shores' fishing villages. Carvalho immediately left for England to continue his PhD program, returning to Brazil in June 1992. He lived in the Capital District of São Paulo until October, when he returned to Fortaleza. Since 1992 the poet has regularly published poems, reviews, chronicles and translations in local publications in *Fortaleza* (especially "afinidades eletivas" and "min"). His first book of poems, *Até a próxima chuva,* is about to be published.

CLAUDIA ROQUETTE-PINTO
Born in Rio de Janeiro in 1963. At the age of seventeen she lived for seven months in San Francisco, CA, completing a course in English and American Studies at San Francisco State University. Back in Brazil, she worked for a while in the fashion industry, first as a model and afterwards as an assistant fashion producer. After graduating in Literary Translation at Pontifícia Universidade Católica in 1987, she worked as a photographer for an architectural firm. From 1986 to 1991 she managed *Verve,* a monthly dedicated to literature and the arts, which she had originally founded with four college friends. She is married, has three children and has published two books of poetry: *Os Dias Gagos* (author's edition, 1991) and *Saxifraga* (Ed. Salamandra, 1993).

Notes composed by Regina Alfarano

SUN & MOON CLASSICS

PIERRE ALFERI [France]
Natural Gaits 95 (1-55713-231-3, $10.95)
The Familiar Path of the Fighting Fish [in preparation]

CLAES ANDERSSON [Finland]
What Became Words 121 (1-55713-231-3, $11.95)

DAVID ANTIN [USA]
Death in Venice: Three Novellas [in preparation]
Selected Poems: 1963–1973 10 (1-55713-058-2, $13.95)

ECE AYHAN [Turkey]
A Blind Cat AND *Orthodoxies* 125 (1-55713-102-3, $10.95)

DJUNA BARNES [USA]
Ann Portuguise [in preparation]
The Antiphon [in preparation]
At the Roots of the Stars: The Short Plays 53 (1-55713-160-0, $12.95)
Biography of Julie von Bartmann [in preparation]
The Book of Repulsive Women 59 (1-55713-173-2, $6.95)
Collected Stories 110 (1-55713-226-7, $24.95 [cloth])
Interviews 86 (0-940650-37-1, $12.95)
New York 5 (0-940650-99-1, $12.95)
Smoke and Other Early Stories 2 (1-55713-014-0, $9.95)

CHARLES BERNSTEIN [USA]
Content's Dream: Essays 1975–1984 49 (0-940650-56-8, $14.95)
Dark City 48 (1-55713-162-7, $11.95)
Republics of Reality: 1975–1995 [in preparation]
Rough Trades 14 (1-55713-080-9, $10.95)

JENS BJØRNEBOE [Norway]
The Bird Lovers 43 (1-55713-146-5, $9.95)
Semmelweis [in preparation]

ANDRÉ DU BOUCHET [France]
The Indwelling [in preparation]
Today the Day [in preparation]
Where Heat Looms 87 (1-55713-238-0, $12.95)

ANDRÉ BRETON [France]
Arcanum 17 51 (1-55713-170-8, $12.95)
Earthlight 26 (1-55713-095-7, $12.95)

DAVID BROMIGE [b. England/Canada]
The Harbormaster of Hong Kong 32 (1-55713-027-2, $10.95)
My Poetry [in preparation]

MARY BUTTS [England]
Scenes from the Life of Cleopatra 72 (1-55713-140-6, $13.95)

OLIVIER CADIOT [France]
Art Poétique [in preparation]

PAUL CELAN [b. Bukovina/France]
Breathturn 74 (1-55713-218-6, $12.95)

LOUIS-FERDINAND CÉLINE [France]
Dances without Music, without Dancers, without Anything
[in preparation]

CLARK COOLIDGE [USA]
The Crystal Text 99 (1-55713-230-5, $11.95)
Own Face 39 (1-55713-120-1, $10.95)
The Rova Improvisations 34 (1-55713-149-x, $11.95)
Solution Passage: Poems 1978–1981 [in preparation]
This Time We Are One/City in Regard [in preparation]

ROSITA COPIOLI [Italy]
The Blazing Lights of the Sun 84 (1-55713-195-3, $11.95)

RENÉ CREVEL [France]
Are You Crazy? [in preparation]
Babylon 65 (1-55713-196-1, $12.95)
Difficult Death [in preparation]

MILO DE ANGELIS [Italy]
Finite Intuition: Selected Poetry and Prose 65 (1-55713-068-x, $11.95)

HENRI DELUY [France]
Carnal Love 121 (1-55713-272-0, $11.95)

RAY DIPALMA [USA]
The Advance on Mesmer [in preparation]
Numbers and Tempers: Selected Early Poems 24
  (1-55713-099-x, $11.95)

HEIMITO VON DODERER [Austria]
The Demons 13 (1-55713-030-2, $29.95)
Every Man a Murderer 66 (1-55713-183-x, $14.95)
The Merowingians 80 (1-55713-250-x, $15.95)

JOSÉ DONOSO [Chile]
Hell Has No Limits 101 (1-55713-187-2, $10.95)

ARKADII DRAGOMOSCHENKO [Russia]
Description 9 (1-55713-075-2, $11.95)
Phosphor [in preparation]
Xenia 29 (1-55713-107-4, $12.95)

JOSÉ MARIA DE EÇA DE QUEIROZ [Portugal]
The City and the Mountains [in preparation]
The Mandarins [in preparation]

LARRY EIGNER [USA]
readiness / enough / depends / on [in preparation]

RAYMOND FEDERMAN [b. France/USA]
Smiles on Washington Square 60 (1-55713-181-3, $10.95)
The Twofold Vibration [in preparation]

RONALD FIRBANK [England]
Santal 58 (1-55713-174-0, $7.95)

DOMINIQUE FOURCADE [France]
Click-Rose 94 (1-55713-264-x, $10.95)
Xbo 35 (1-55713-067-1, $9.95)

SIGMUND FREUD [Austria]
Delusion and Dream in Wilhelm Jensen's GRADIVA 38
  (1-55713-139-2, $11.95)

MAURICE GILLIAMS [Belgium/Flanders]
Elias, or The Struggle with the Nightingales 79 (1-55713-206-2, $12.95)

LILIANE GIRAUDON [France]
Fur 114 (1-55713-222-4, $12.95)
Pallaksch, Pallaksch 61 (1-55713-191-0, $12.95)

ALFREDO GIULIANI [Italy]
Ed. *I Novissimi: Poetry for the Sixties* 55
  (1-55713-137-6, $14.95)
Verse and Nonverse [in preparation]

TED GREENWALD [USA]
Going into School that Day [in preparation]
Licorice Chronicles [in preparation]

BARBARA GUEST [USA]
Defensive Rapture 30 (1-55713-032-9, $11.95)
Fair Realism 41 (1-55713-245-3, $10.95)
Moscow Mansions [in preparation]
Seeking Air [in preparation]
Selected Poems [in preparation]

HERVÉ GUIBERT [France]
Ghost Image 93 (1-55713-276-4, $13.95)

KNUT HAMSUN [Norway]
Rosa [in preparation]
Under the Autumn Star [in preparation]
Victoria 69 (1-55713-177-5, $10.95)
Wayfarers 88 (1-55713-211-9, $13.95)
The Wanderer Plays on Muted Strings [in preparation]
The Women at the Pump 115 (1-55713-244-5, $14.95)

MARTIN A. HANSEN [Denmark]
The Liar 111 (1-55713-243-7, $12.95)

THOMAS HARDY [England]
Jude the Obscure 77 (1-55713-203-8, $12.95)

PAAL-HELGE HAUGEN [Norway]
Wintering with the Light 107 (1-55713-273-9, $10.95)

MARIANNE HAUSER [b. Alsace-Lorraine/USA]
The Long and the Short: Selected Stories [in preparation]
Me & My Mom 36 (1-55713-175-9, $9.95)
Prince Ishmael 4 (1-55713-039-6, $11.95)

JOHN HAWKES [USA]
The Owl AND *The Goose on the Grave* 67 (1-55713-194-5, $12.95)

LYN HEJINIAN [USA]
The Cell 21 (1-55713-021-3, $11.95)
The Cold of Poetry 42 (1-55713-063-9, $12.95)
My Life 11 (1-55713-024-8, $9.95)
Writing Is an Aid to Memory 141 (1-55713-271-2, $9.95)

EMMANUEL HOCQUARD [France]
The Cape of Good Hope [in preparation]

SIGURD HOEL [Norway]
The Road to the World's End 75 (1-55713-210-0, $13.95)

FANNY HOWE [USA]
The Deep North 15 (1-55713-105-8, $9.95)
Radical Love: A Trilogy [in preparation]
Saving History 27 (1-55713-100-7, $12.95)

SUSAN HOWE [USA]
The Europe of Trusts 7 (1-55713-009-4, $10.95)

LAURA (RIDING) JACKSON [USA]
Lives of Wives 71 (1-55713-182-1, $12.95)

HENRY JAMES [USA]
The Awkward Age [in preparation]
What Maisie Knew [in preparation]

LEN JENKIN [USA]
Dark Ride and Other Plays 22 (1-55713-073-6, $13.95)
Careless Love 54 (1-55713-168-6, $9.95)
Pilgrims of the Night: Five Plays [in preparation]

WILHELM JENSEN [Germany]
Gradiva 38 (1-55713-139-2, $13.95)

JEFFREY M. JONES [USA]
The Crazy Plays and Others [in preparation]
J. P. Morgan Saves the Nation 157 (1-55713-256-9, $9.95)
Love Trouble 78 (1-55713-198-8, $9.95)
Night Coil [in preparation]

STEVE KATZ [USA]
Florry of Washington Heights [in preparation]
43 Fictions 18 (1-55713-069-8, $12.95)
Swanny's Ways [in preparation]
Wier & Pouce [in preparation]

ALEXEI KRUCHENYKH [Russia]
Suicide Circus: Selected Poems [in preparation]

THOMAS LA FARGE [USA]
Terror of Earth 136 (1-55713-261-5, $11.95)

VALERY LARBAUD [France]
Childish Things 19 (1-55713-119-8, $13.95)

OSMAN LINS [Brazil]
Nine, Novena 104 (1-55713-229-1, $12.95)

NATHANIEL MACKEY [USA]
Bedouin Hornbook [in preparation]

JACKSON MAC LOW [USA]
Barnesbook 127 (1-55713-235-6, $9.95)
From Pearl Harbor Day to FDR's Birthday 126
  (0-940650-19-3, $10.95)
Pieces O' Six 17 (1-55713-060-4, $11.95)
Two Plays [in preparation]

CLARENCE MAJOR [USA]
Painted Turtle: Woman with Guitar (1-55713-085-X, $11.95)

F. T. MARINETTI [Italy]
Let's Murder the Moonshine: Selected Writings 12
(1-55713-101-5, $13.95)
The Untameables 28 (1-55713-044-7, $10.95)

HARRY MATHEWS [USA]
Selected Declarations of Dependence (1-55713-234-8, $10.95)

FRIEDRIKE MAYRÖCKER [Austria]
with each clouded peak [in preparation]

DOUGLAS MESSERLI [USA]
After [in preparation]
Ed. *50: A Celebration of Sun & Moon Classics* 50
(1-55713-132-5, $13.95)
Ed. *From the Other Side of the Century: A New American
Poetry 1960–1990* 47 (1-55713-131-7, $29.95)
Ed. [with Mac Wellman] *From the Other Side of the
Century II: A New American Drama 1960–1995* [in preparation]
River to Rivet: A Poetic Trilogy [in preparation]

DAVID MILLER [England]
The River of Marah [in preparation]

CHRISTOPHER MORLEY [USA]
Thunder on the Left 68 (1-55713-190-2, $12.95)

GÉRARD DE NERVAL [France]
Aurelia [in preparation]

VALÈRE NOVARINA [France]
The Theater of the Ears 85 (1-55713-251-8, $13.95)

CHARLES NORTH [USA]
New and Selected Poems [in preparation]

TOBY OLSON [USA]
Dorit in Lesbos [in preparation]
Utah [in preparation]

MAGGIE O'SULLIVAN [England]
Palace of Reptiles [in preparation]

SERGEI PARADJANOV [Armenia]
Seven Visions [in preparation]

ANTONIO PORTA [Italy]
Metropolis [in preparation]

ANTHONY POWELL [England]
Afternoon Men [in preparation]
Agents and Patients [in preparation]
From a View to a Death [in preparation]
O, How the Wheel Becomes It! 76 (1-55713-221-6, $10.95)
Venusburg [in preparation]
What's Become of Waring [in preparation]

SEXTUS PROPERTIUS [Ancient Rome]
Charm 89 (1-55713-224-0, $11.95)

RAYMOND QUENEAU [France]
Children of Clay [in preparation]

CARL RAKOSI [USA]
Poems 1923–1941 64 (1-55713-185-6, $12.95)

TOM RAWORTH [England]
Eternal Sections 23 (1-55713-129-5, $9.95)

NORBERTO LUIS ROMERO [Spain]
The Arrival of Autumn in Constantinople [in preparation]

AMELIA ROSSELLI [Italy]
War Variations [in preparation]

JEROME ROTHENBERG [USA]
Gematria 45 (1-55713-097-3, $11.95)

SEVERO SARDUY [Cuba]
From Cuba with a Song 52 (1-55713-158-9, $10.95)

ALBERTO SAVINIO [Italy]
Selected Stories [in preparation]

LESLIE SCALAPINO [USA]
Defoe 46 (1-55713-163-5, $14.95)

ARTHUR SCHNITZLER [Austria]
Dream Story 6 (1-55713-081-7, $11.95)
Lieutenant Gustl 37 (1-55713-176-7, $9.95)

GILBERT SORRENTINO [USA]
The Orangery 91 (1-55713-225-9, $10.95)

ADRIANO SPATOLA [Italy]
Collected Poetry [in preparation]

GERTRUDE STEIN [USA]
How to Write 83 (1-55713-204-6, $12.95)
Mrs. Reynolds 1 (1-55713-016-7, $13.95)
Stanzas in Meditation 44 (1-55713-169-4, $11.95)
Tender Buttons 8 (1-55713-093-0, $9.95)
To Do [in preparation]
Winning His Way and Other Poems [in preparation]

GIUSEPPE STEINER [Italy]
Drawn States of Mind 63 (1-55713-171-6, $8.95)

ROBERT STEINER [USA]
Bathers [in preparation]
The Catastrophe 134 (1-55713-232-1, $26.95 [cloth])

JOHN STEPPLING [USA]
Sea of Cortez and Other Plays 96 (1-55713-237-2, $14.95)

STIJN STREUVELS [Belgium/Flanders]
The Flaxfield 3 (1-55713-050-7, $11.95)

ITALO SVEVO [Italy]
As a Man Grows Older 25 (1-55713-128-7, $12.95)

JOHN TAGGART [USA]
Crosses [in preparation]
Loop 150 (1-55713-012-4, $11.95)

FIONA TEMPLETON [Scotland]
Delirium of Interpretations [in preparation]

SUSANA THÉNON [Argentina]
distancias / distances 40 (1-55713-153-8, $10.95)

JALAL TOUFIC [Lebanon]
Over-Sensitivity 119 (1-55713-270-4, $13.95)

TCHICAYA U TAM'SI [The Congo]
The Belly [in preparation]

PAUL VAN OSTAIJEN [Belgium/Flanders]
The First Book of Schmoll [in preparation]

CARL VAN VECHTEN [USA]
Parties 31 (1-55713-029-9, $13.95)
Peter Whiffle [in preparation]

TARJEI VESAAS [Norway]
The Great Cycle [in preparation]
The Ice Palace 16 (1-55713-094-9, $11.95)

KEITH WALDROP [USA]
The House Seen from Nowhere [in preparation]
Light While There Is Light: An American History 33
   (1-55713-136-8, $13.95)

WENDY WALKER [USA]
The Sea-Rabbit or, The Artist of Life 57 (1-55713-001-9, $12.95)
The Secret Service 20 (1-55713-084-1, $13.95)
Stories Out of Omarie 58 (1-55713-172-4, $12.95)

BARRETT WATTEN [USA]
Frame (1971–1991) 117 (1-55713-239-9, $13.95)

MAC WELLMAN [USA]
The Land Beyond the Forest: Dracula AND *Swoop* 112
   (1-55713-228-3, $12.95)
The Land of Fog and Whistles: Selected Plays [in preparation]
Two Plays: A Murder of Crows AND *The Hyacinth Macaw* 62
   (1-55713-197-X, $11.95)

JOHN WIENERS [USA]
707 Scott Street 106 (1-55713-252-6, $12.95)

ÉMILE ZOLA [France]
The Belly of Paris 70 (1-55713-066-3, $14.95)